MECHANICS-
MERCANTILE
LIBRARY.

Arthur F Mathews '06

Longing for
Elsewhere

Longing for Elsewhere
My Irish Voyage Through
Hunger, History and High Times
A Memoir

Library of Congress Control Number: 2011961045

ISBN 978-0-615-55488-4

Cover Design by Kina Sullivan
Interior Design by Kathryn Marcellino

Printed in the United States of America

For My Darlings

Ashling, Lew, Alanna and Ronnie

❧

Paris, 1963.

Longing for Elsewhere

My Irish Voyage Through
Hunger, History and High Times

Renée Gibbons

Table of Contents

꙳

Introduction
Longing for Elsewhere

୬

I have been longing for elsewhere for as far back as I can remember. This constant longing has nudged, elbowed and pushed me at various times to find people and places—not only in the world but within myself—that I have come to love and treasure. I now share those treasures in this book.

This is a collection of stories and vignettes written over many decades. They begin with my family in the Dublin tenement where I grew up as the oldest of seven children. My father's attention was not on his family but on where he could get the money for his next drink and whether the horse he'd backed might win. My mother spent her time being angry at him because of this and we, the children, often got the brunt of it. Daddy would sometimes come home on a Friday night, roll his razor and shaving brush up in the evening paper, put it under his arm, and say he was taking the mail boat to Liverpool to look for work. This usually meant he'd lost his job. Once he had a job delivering coal by horse and cart, and became accustomed to leaving them outside some pub or other while he nipped in for a pint. The day the mare went back to the depot by herself was the day my dad got fired. Whenever he disappeared or even when he stayed home Mammy was left to forage for food as best she could. The main topic of conversation was food and how and where we were going to get it. Everything else was secondary.

I knew I didn't want the life my parents had, and daydreaming became my way of escaping reality. I could spend hours looking off into the middle distance, imagining all the beautiful, faraway places I'd heard about from storybooks.

When I was eleven we were evicted from our tenement and the family was moved to a part of Dublin that had become known as Hell's Half Acre. But by then I was starting to build a new life for myself and was rarely home. I escaped into music and theatre and endless dreams of travel, and started spending time with artists and intellectuals near the center of the city. At seventeen I escaped to Paris with the help of a nun, a Hollywood actor and a kind stranger. There I was accepted into the community of actors, writers and musicians who had been blacklisted during the McCarthy era. I met James Baldwin and Ring Lardner Jr., Hilaire Hiler and his daughter DeDe, actress and writer Ruth Gordon and the actor William Marshall.

In my own mind, though, I was still the little girl from the Dublin slums. I returned to Ireland, got pregnant, and gave my son up for adoption. A couple of years later another unplanned pregnancy threw me over the edge. I spent the next seven years wandering in the wilderness, as it were, all around the world, trying to find out where I belonged and what it all meant. I very consciously decided to have a child at that point, and gave birth to my darling daughter, Aisling. On a ship bound from Vancouver to Egypt when Aisling was just a year old, I met and fell in love with a radical longshoreman from San Francisco. Lew and I are still married, thirty-six years later.

The Bohemian city of San Francisco is now my home base, but I still long for elsewhere. I wonder if someday I will live in Paris again, or in a small Tibetan inn by a lake in the Himalayas, or perhaps in a wee cottage in the west of Ireland.

The habit of longing dies hard, but I know myself now and see the richness my longing has brought to my life. The ability to imagine, to fantasize is what has kept me from getting depressed or maudlin. I suppose if you can imagine a better life, fantasize about something beautiful in the midst of poverty, long for love when you feel its absence—then you have hope.

Here's to love, to life!

Part 1
My Parents

&

We all begin with our parents, and mine were a colorful pair. As a child, I could only react to them—for better or worse. As I grew older and came to understand myself better, I also understood them better too. My mother Rosie held the family together, but she had an awful temper and goaded my dad into many of his transgressions. My father Paddy was a terrible alcoholic, but loved us desperately even as he made our lives more difficult. In the end, I was blessed to reconcile with both of them and to realize how much I loved them—and how much they loved me.

Where It All Started

૨

Our family lived in Verschoyle Place in Dublin, a lane made up of tenement buildings. Three other families lived in our building, one above us and two across the hall from us. We had no indoor plumbing; instead, there was a concrete backyard with two outdoor toilets and a tap for running water. Across the backyard were more tenement buildings that fronted out toward Stephen's Lane. Six families, sometimes more, shared the two toilets and one water tap.

These two lanes were sandwiched between the grand Georgian houses of Upper Mount Street and Lower Mount Street. We were less than a mile from Nelson's Pillar, the heart of the city.

As far as I know, four generations of my family had lived in Verschoyle Place. My great grandmother, Biddy Redmond, had come from County Wexford and married Michael Murphy, a jarvey who drove a horse and carriage. Rumor had it that before moving to Dublin, Biddy had been a lady-in-waiting in the home of Lord Edward Fitzgerald. This may be a bit of romanticizing on someone's part, because I've heard other Irish people tell the same tale. Perhaps it makes the bitter reality of poverty and hunger easier to handle. Lords and ladies who have fallen on hard times make a better story than poor, landless peasants with little hope of digging their way out of the slums.

When I was very young, I didn't know that I was poor and living in a slum. I was a happy child by all accounts. At least, that's how I appeared to others. I was very curious. It didn't take me long to notice the difference between the front of Mount Street and the back of it where we lived, and the difference between the living conditions of the rich and the poor.

Mammy was the breadwinner in the family and often worked for people who were well off. She would cook or clean or do whatever jobs she could get. Sometimes when she was working in a posh house nearby, I would bring the latest baby around in the pram for her to nurse, and then take the baby home again. That gave me a chance to see the inside of some of the grander houses. These were not the houses of the very rich, just people who were much better off than we were.

Daddy was often away. If he wasn't working in England, he'd be in the pub drinking with his mates until closing time. On Friday nights, Mammy would chase around the pubs looking for him to see if he had any money left from his pay-packet or the dole.

I started school before I was four years old. I suppose the nuns in the parochial school felt sorry for Mammy and allowed me to start earlier than usual. It might seem like a punishment to some people to be packed off to regular school at such a tender age, but to me it was more of an adventure. Mammy had her hands full with another toddler at home and a third child on the way. Daddy was off somewhere in England again, supposedly looking for work. He gravitated there because there were more jobs and because he'd been in the British Army, even if he had gone AWOL.

I liked school because my teacher, Miss McDonnell, was very fond of me and treated me well. She sat in a wheelchair at the front of the class, which was quite intriguing. I never knew why she had to use the wheelchair. What I remember most about her is that she was never angry. Almost every grownup I knew seemed to be angry, and I knew that angry people could hurt you. I had learned to be hyper-vigilant, aware of everything that went on around me. I heard even the quietest whisper. Mammy said I could hear the grass grow.

I adored my mother, but she had a temper. One morning Mammy and Mrs. Lawless, our neighbor across the hall, had a terrible fight. It started because Mrs. Lawless said something bad about me or my brother, and Mammy pulled her hair. Then they really started hitting each other—so hard that Mammy had to get a steak and hold it to her face so she wouldn't have a black eye the next day, for everyone to see. I don't know where she got that steak, because we never had steak to eat.

Mammy could be both mean and sentimental, often in quick succession. One day she sent one of my younger sisters, Fiona, to the pawn shop with a bundle of clothes to exchange for money. Mammy sat waiting for her to get back so she could buy some bread and milk—and if there was enough left over, maybe a can of beans or a few sausages to feed her hungry brood. Fiona had been sent because she was a precocious nine-year-old and more likely than any of the rest of us to haggle for a larger sum of money with John the pawnbroker.

She arrived home much later than expected and presented our mother with a gift—a framed sentimental poem entitled "Mother" sitting on a small, silver-colored stand. She had seen it in a shop window on her way home, and the roses painted around the edges caught her eye because our mother's name was Rose. Mammy became a very thorny rose when Fiona told her she had spent all the money on that gift. In a fit of rage, she broke the ornament over my sister's head. Fiona had no idea what she had done wrong.

I was thirteen at the time and understood we needed bread more than we needed poetry. But for years and years afterwards, without another word being spoken about the incident, the mended ornament with the poem "Mother" enjoyed a prominent place on our mantelpiece.

Mammy's temper could be directed towards me as well. One day when I was eight or nine years old, and one of the children was sick, she sent me next door to the corner shop to buy lemonade. We only had lemonade in the house if someone was sick. "Get the Taylor-Keith brand, not the Savage-Smith," she kept saying over and over until my head was ready to explode. I went next door and, in my confusion, bought the wrong brand.

She was furious. She sat me down in a chair and hit me over the head with that glass bottle of lemonade! The pain in my heart was worse than the pain from the lump on my head. Mammy who loved and adored me, and who was loved and adored in return, had hit me. The person I loved most in the world had turned on me. I felt stranded. Daddy already felt lost to me. He had been going back and forth to England, and I'd shut him out of my heart because I couldn't bear the pain.

That was the day I lost my innocence. I knew then that there was no one to trust but myself, and that I shouldn't ask anything or tell anything—except maybe to my brother Sean.

The Lane

❧

My early life was lived in poverty, but it was not joyless. We had beauty, humor, and adventure as well. My brothers and sisters and I loved to plan break-ins of the local grocery stores. We never carried them out. We weren't criminals. It was just play-acting to take our minds off being hungry. We loved describing how we'd spend our winnings from the Irish Hospitals' Sweepstakes, even though we never had a ticket.

We had a lot of music in our lives. Mammy and Daddy were both lovely singers, and we had records to play and music on the radio—even though sometimes the beauty might be short-lived. Mammy and Daddy might be singing love duets one minute, and the next minute he might lash out and punch her.

There were lots of other children to play with in the lane. Most women had a child every year or so, hence the term "Irish twins." My brother Sean came along fifteen months after me. Mammy said that when she brought him home from Holles Street Maternity Hospital, I hit him over the head with my rubber duck. It surprised me to hear that I'd even had a rubber duck.

We poor kids never had shop bought toys, so we invented games and played with scavenged materials. Kathleen McLaughlin was my best friend. She had a piece of red velvet that we draped over the smelly toilet seat in her tenement, and made it a throne for queens and princesses. Her older sister, Betty, sometimes loaned us hair ornaments and perfume. We made up a game called Shop. We would dig in derelict building sites for broken china and glass, and weigh them on improvised scales. Gold-rimmed china and blue glass were the most desirable, and we'd trade each other for the fancier pieces. We would walk around with tin cans tied to our feet and pretend we were on stilts. Empty shoe polish cans with a length of twine became telephones or walkie-talkies.

Summertime was our favorite season because we could forage for free food. Blackberries grew in every nook and cranny, and on the long summer nights at low tide we'd go to Sandymount Strand and dig for cockles. On the way home, we might box-the-fox (in other words steal a few apples from someone's back garden).

Some nights, we'd create a theatre in the yard between the tenements by stringing a clothes line between some poles, throwing a heavy blanket over it for a curtain, and arranging some orange crates or tea-chests in a circle for the audience to sit on. We'd dress up, act out skits and sing some songs. Mag McGowran lived in the tenement next door. She'd been an actress at one time and had lots of stage make-up that she let us use. The boys would dress as girls and the girls would be the heroes. We'd charge an entrance fee of a halfpenny or a penny, and afterwards we'd buy lemonade and sweets and everyone would share the goodies.

We were lucky to have the lane to play in, for it was safe to run in the streets and stay out late at night. We only came home to see if there was anything to eat and to go to bed.

Despite the good times, though, what I mostly remember about the early days is the talk about food and how we had none. Winters were hard. Mammy would try to find work in a restaurant so she could take home leftover food, and occasionally steal a ham or lump of cheese and tie it to her body inside her clothes. Mammy's chief occupation was trying to feed her children. She had no pride when it came to begging for food for us, whether from the St. Vincent De Paul Society or the soup kitchens for the poor. On days when she had to send us off to school hungry, she'd find something to pawn and bring some biscuits or a snack by school to tide us over until we got home. Sometimes dinner consisted of only a few tomatoes, onions, and a watered down Oxo cube. Together with a slice of bread and cup of tea, this made a scrumptious meal.

And more children kept arriving. After Sean came Patricia (who changed her name to Kala), then Fiona, Gemma, and Veronica. We were eight people living in two rooms. (Little Patrick wouldn't arrive for another six years after Veronica.) We slept four to a bed. We had a gas cooker and an open fireplace. The front room was kept for "good" and was rarely used. The back room, where we lived, had a concrete floor covered with linoleum.

We had gas lamps for lighting, and often we couldn't pay the gas bill so the power would be cut off. When that happened, we'd have to cook in the fireplace. If we didn't have coal or turf, we'd burn old shoes. The food became smoky and smutty, but we ate it anyway. The gas meter had to be fed with coins. One of us would break open the lock on the meter and we'd use the same coin over and over again. If we didn't have a coin, we'd cut small pieces of linoleum into the size and shape of a coin and use that. When the gas man came around to empty the meter, he'd either find nothing inside or it would be filled with those little linoleum chips. In either case, we were cut off immediately. So for the most part, we had no gas.

The bills just kept mounting. Daddy would be away in England looking for work and Mammy felt the strain of being responsible for everything. She told all her troubles to me and Sean, and we felt a responsibility to the younger children. Sean had odd jobs from the time he was six or seven, helping the bread delivery man or cleaning out a pigsty for a man in our lane. My contribution was asking my teachers, "Can you help my daddy find a job?" Sometimes they did, but he never kept them because he got drunk all the time.

Daddy only looked after us when Mammy was in hospital getting us a new sister or brother. I was always surprised when she came home with a baby. No one talked about where babies came from, and I was completely innocent. While Mammy was away, Daddy would feed us on crisps, marshmallows and bottles of Bulmer's Cidona, an apple drink. He knew a man who owned a sweets factory, so we also had lots of candy during Mammy's absence. Daddy had no idea how to cook.

My brother Sean and I learned early on to be resourceful. Sometimes we succeeded, and sometimes we did not. Once when Mammy was in hospital getting another baby, he and I went to the parish priest's house. We told him we were hungry and asked for something to eat. I said, "Mammy is in hospital and Daddy is in the pub drinking all the money."

The priest was impatient with us, and I remember him jangling some change in his pockets. Finally he shouted, "Don't be speaking ill of your father. It would suit you better to go home and obey your father and your mother." He shut the door in our faces without offering us a crumb. That was the beginning of my disillusionment with religion and the clergy.

After my brother and I licked our wounds, we went to our next door neighbor and asked if she had any stale bread "to feed the ducks in St. Stephen's Green." She gave us a bag of old bread. We soaked it in a basin of water, fried it up in drippings, and sprinkled salt on it.

We didn't feel guilty about not feeding the ducks. We knew they were better fed than we were.

Mammy's Early Dreams

I asked Mammy once how she met my father. She told me she'd had no interest in Paddy Jackson when she was growing up, even though they had known one another as children and lived in adjacent lanes.

Mammy was a beautiful young woman with lots of friends, a good job as a bookbinder with Brown and Nolan, and a busy social life. She enjoyed playing field hockey, going to the races and soccer matches. She was a lovely singer and designed and made her own clothes, including fabulous hats.

She was twenty-four and on the rebound from a romance with Jack Kenny when Paddy Jackson thought he might try his chances with the local beauty. He was a charming rascal, by all accounts, and Rosie capitulated. Mammy said they married right away and he moved into the two tenement rooms she shared with her granny, Biddy Murphy.

Mammy went to work after the marriage, and the dreams and romance faded from her life. She told me that once when she was scrubbing the steps outside a fancy Georgian house on Stephen's Green, some of the girls from her hockey playing days walked by. She covered her face in shame and embarrassment, and later wept at the thought of how hard her life had become. She isolated herself from her old friends and concentrated all her energy on looking after her kids. She cooked, cleaned, knit, sewed, scrubbed and did laundry for anyone who would hire her.

She'd had dreams of a glamorous life. She had style and beauty and talent. She entered beauty contests in the hopes that, like Maureen O'Hara, she might be picked out of a line-up and offered a career in Hollywood. But it was not to be.

This Is My Father

❧

"Children begin by loving their parents. After a time, they judge them. Rarely, if ever, do they forgive them." I've always loved that quote from Oscar Wilde.

Loving my father was easy when I was little. I have a photograph of the two of us when I was about two and he was twenty-eight. We look like we are completely in love with one another. The picture was taken in front of a little huckster shop in the lane where we lived. My hair is snow white—"Snowball" was my nickname—and I am wearing some homemade clothes, lacy socks and shoes with ankle straps. My father's hair, in contrast, is jet black and very wavy. He is sharply dressed in slacks, sports jacket, shirt and tie. I can't see his shoes, but I know they are the shiniest ones on earth for he polished them compulsively. We both have large eyes and his hand is on my hand. Our hands are identical except for the difference in size. My father could never disclaim me.

I was his first child. Mammy told me the story of the day I was born. She was in Holles Street Maternity Hospital and asked Daddy to go and buy her the lemon drops she was craving. Somewhere along the way, he ran into his mate Jack Nail, who had just gotten a tip on a horse running in the 3:30 at Leopardstown. They didn't have a penny between them to back the horse, but my father noticed that Jack Nail was wearing a new pair of shoes. Next thing you know, they were in Brereton's pawn shop pawning the new shoes. Jack Nail came out in his bare feet and the two of them went to the bookie to back the horse. It came in at ten to one and, needless to say, my mother and the lemon drops were forgotten as the two men got ossified spending their winnings in the local pub, The Hive. Jack Nail's wife shouted at him about that for the next year and Mammy never let my father forget that he was AWOL the day of my birth.

Still, I was the apple of his eye and he used to take me out to show me off. We would go to "the drunkards' Mass" at Mespil Road Church in Dublin, so called because it was the latest Mass on Sunday morning and the congregation usually overflowed out onto the sidewalk. There my father would meet up with his drinking buddies from the night before and make sure everyone had a chance to see his beautiful daughter. He was the center of my universe. I felt completely secure in his love, but it didn't last. Before long he took off for England.

Judging my father became easy as I moved out of childhood innocence into adolescence. He failed to provide for his family. On top of that, a new baby arrived every year or two and he spent more time in the pubs and left my mother to manage as best she could.

Some of my very earliest memories are of running alongside Mammy as she pushed the pram with two or three kids in it from pub to pub, trying to find Daddy in hopes of catching him while he still had a few shillings left. I can still hear the wheels of the pram on the cobblestones, feel the rain on my head and the smell of piss in the alleyways. Often Daddy's mates would lie and say they had not seen him, and we would go home empty-handed and Mammy in tears.

He had a habit of coming home drunk on Friday nights with *The Evening Herald* tucked under his arm. He would unfold it, put his razor, shaving brush, toothbrush and toothpaste inside the newspaper and announce, "I am taking the mail boat to England to look for work."

I would cry, hug his legs and beg him, "Daddy, don't go." He would disappear for months or years, I couldn't tell how long, and I began to shut him out of my affections. I just couldn't stand the pain of losing him over and over.

Life with my father got worse as I got older. By the time I left home at seventeen, it had become a nightmare. He spiraled downward into alcoholism and violence, and became a punitive, nasty husband and father. Every night, we waited in fear of another drunken drama when he arrived home after the pubs closed. I sometimes dreamed of ways to kill him.

One night he threw a coat I was knitting onto the burning fireplace. I gave him "some lip," as he called it. We kept by the fireplace one of those very heavy, old-fashioned irons that you had to heat over a fire to iron clothes. He picked it up and flung it across the room at me. My mother jumped in front of me to save me from getting hit, and the iron knocked her unconscious. I thought she was dead. I got on my knees, crying and begging her not to die. An ambulance was called and she was taken to hospital, where she stayed for ten days.

Later that week while Mammy was in the hospital, I tried to kill my father. I knew a policeman who had a girlfriend who worked at a hospital, and I knew he fancied me. I flirted with him so I could ask him to get me a bottle of barbiturates through his girlfriend. One night Daddy came home filthy drunk. My sister Gemma, who idolized him, was fixing some chicken noodle soup for him and I emptied the bottle of pills into his bowl. I didn't wait for him to die. I just high-tailed it out of there and caught the very next boat and train to England.

My dad didn't die; he just slept for seventy-two hours. I didn't know that, though. In any case, I was confident that had I killed him, I would get away with it. Hadn't he tried to kill me and almost killed my mother?

Music

ꝏ

My father loved opera. He had a beautiful voice and could sing all the famous Italian operatic arias in a kind of phonetic made-up Italian. My mother sang, too, and they had favorite duets they sang together. One was "Girls Were Made to Love and Kiss." They also loved "This is My Lovely Day" and "Stranger in Paradise."

In the early days of my parents' marriage, they entered amateur talent contests for cash prizes. We had an old-fashioned HMV record player and scads of 78s. We had Gigli, Caruso, Bjorling, and many others. Besides opera, we had the records of Paul Robeson, The Weavers, Nat King Cole, and all the Broadway musicals.

I was about eight when the record player and all the records disappeared from our front room. My mother accused my father of pawning them to buy drink. It was probably true, but she could just as easily have pawned them herself to buy food. That was how our household operated. Once a thing went into the pawn shop, we rarely saw it again because there was never any money to redeem it. Luckily, we still had the radio and could listen to the BBC and Radio Eireann.

Daddy checked the obituaries every day and went to funerals and wakes whether or not he knew the deceased. Once there, he traded his wit for drinks. He'd do anything to get a drink, even sell his platelets and offer himself up as a guinea pig for new drug trials. (If you donated a pint of blood in Ireland, you were rewarded with a pint of Guinness.) If he didn't have the price of a drink, he'd order me out to ask a neighbor for a loan of a shilling or two. Then he'd buy five Woodbine cigarettes and go to the bookmaker's and back a horse.

He was always waiting for his horse to win, for his ship to come in and dreamed endlessly of what he would do with his winnings. What he did do, in fact, if the horse won was go to the nearest pub and buy drinks for everyone. He never told Mammy when he backed a winning horse, but we would hear it on the street later on. And there were certain tip-offs. He'd roll down the avenue, singing at the top of his lungs, and stumble into the house singing "Girls Were Made to Love and Kiss." We'd know he'd backed a winner, and that was our cue to roll him for any money he might have left over. He would always tie it into the tail of his shirt. Since he was in no shape to undress himself, Mammy and I would take his shoes and trousers off and put him to bed. I'd be terrified, waiting for him to fall asleep. When we were sure he was completely out, Mammy and I would roll him over to get to the tail of his shirt and take the money.

The next morning he'd say to Mammy, "Jaysus Rosie, I was sure I had a few bob last night when I went to bed." She'd look all innocent and then he'd ask her, "Can you lend me a couple of bob so I can get a pint and back a horse?" She'd give it to him and off he'd go, happy as Larry.

Surprise

❧

Sometimes what seem like small moments can turn into life-changing events.

I made my First Holy Communion at St. Andrew's in Westland Row when I was seven. As I was coming down the steps with all the other girls and boys, a woman with a large collie dog ran up the steps, grabbed me, and hugged and kissed me. She told me I was beautiful. Then, as quick as lightning, she was gone with the dog following behind.

In 1974 I was home in Dublin and Mammy and I were in her kitchen, drinking tea. I was telling her about that incident and how it had always confounded me. I described the woman as best I could and gave a vivid description of the dog.

"Oh! that's Lizzie Kane," Mammy said.

"Is she still alive?" I asked

"Oh yes! She still lives in the lane where she was born and raised. She'd be in her 70s by now. She was your grandmother Nellie's best friend."

The next day I went into Power's Court to find her. When she opened the door, she looked me up and down and said, "I think I know who you are. Are you Renée Jackson? My God, you look very like Elwyn."

I reminded her of the incident at my First Holy Communion and told her I had come to find out something about Nellie. Off she went and returned with a photograph from an old shoe box. She handed it to me and said, "This is me and Nellie with Betty Jackson, your father's mother, at a dance." In the photo, three Irish beauties about eighteen years old smiled for the camera. "We were best friends, the three of us, you know."

She proceeded to tell me about Nellie and Elwyn. He was an American in the Navy whose ship was docked in Dublin during World War I. Nellie met him at a dance that the three girlfriends attended together. "Nellie became pregnant," Lizzie Kane said. "I could never conceive, or I'd probably have been pregnant too. All of us had boyfriends from overseas. I never had any children. Elwyn loved Nellie, but her mother Biddy stood in the way of it. She intercepted the letters he wrote and was completely against the relationship. It broke Nellie's heart."

She went on to deliver a second surprise. Betty Jackson had also gotten pregnant by her boyfriend, a British Intelligence Officer.

After I left Lizzie that afternoon, I regretted not having asked her for the photograph of the three best friends. I had never seen a photo of my paternal grandmother, Betty Jackson, and doubted I'd get another chance. On that same visit, my mother gave me a photograph of my grandmother, Nellie Murphy, holding my mother as an infant. It was inscribed, "To Elwyn from your loving Nellie and Rosie." I wondered how my mother had ended up with that photo.

Until that talk with Lizzie Kane I had no idea that my mother's mother and my father's mother had been friends and that both of them had gotten pregnant about the same time. It was a lot to absorb.

Stranded

~

I thought a great deal about my mother and grand-mother after the visit with Lizzie Kane. I let my imagination run away with me and wrote what I thought the scenario might have been surrounding my mother's birth.

It was October 1919. Nineteen-year-old Nellie Murphy had just finished her porridge and cup of tea when she felt a terrific urge to be near the sea. She made a sandwich and decided to take a walk to Sandymount Strand.

"I must wash my hair before I set off," she said to herself as she sat by the blazing fire with its kettle of perpetually boiling water. Nellie washed her hair and toweled it dry. She put on her best hat, the green one that matched her eyes, grabbed her brown wool coat from the back of the door and headed out.

"Where are you off to?" her mother Biddy asked.

"I fancy taking a walk to Sandymount Strand and back," Nellie replied.

"Mind you don't catch your death of cold and it nearly November," her mother called after her.

Nellie set off, her damp wavy hair cascading down her back, the green hat tilted at an angle. She buttoned up her coat against the chill October day and made her way through Eblana Villas and Ringsend to Sandymount. When she reached the Strand, she took off her high-button boots and walked barefoot in the sand. Her mother would kill her if she knew. The sea air made her ravenous, so she ate her sardine sandwich right away and sat on the sea wall watching the sun battle the rain-laden clouds. The sun won out and she was there to witness and enjoy every minute of it. She felt so lonely all of a sudden. She rummaged through her purse 'til she found the small oval photograph. It showed a handsome young man in uniform and was signed, "To my darling Nellie."

She wondered why she hadn't received any letters from him lately. He'd told her he loved her and would take care of her.

A fine mist rose off the bay and she felt a chill run through her. She thought to herself that someone had just walked on her grave. Perhaps it was time to head home. The sun would be going down soon and then the cold would really set in. It was only a mile to walk, but she wished she'd asked her mother for a halfpenny to catch the tram back to Mount Street.

She walked along the Grand Canal past Boland's bakery. Jesus, she was starving. It was Halloween, or Samhain, a day for special treats like barm brack and curly kale, and pancakes with sugar and lemon juice, her favorite. The children were already on the streets, their faces blackened with soot.

"Help the Halloween party," they begged.

"Help the Halloween party yourselves," she shouted back.

Samhain was the night when the veil between worlds is thinnest and the souls of the departed roam the earth. Terrible things had been seen in the lane where she lived. Someone had seen a huge ball of fire roll down the street. She herself had heard the clippity-clop of the headless horseman many a Halloween night.

"Jesus, Mary and Joseph, where have you been all this time?" her mother greeted her when she arrived home. "You should be saving all your energy to push that baby of yours out. You must be famished. Sit down and eat."

In the middle of the meal, Nellie felt herself sitting in a pool of warm water on the chair.

"It's your time, daughter," her mother said gently and shouted upstairs for Mrs. Kavanagh in the top tenement. The big iron tub was brought in from the back yard and extra kettles of water were set boiling on the fire. A couple of the neighborhood women, mid-wives in their own right, were sent for and Nellie moaned as the contractions started in earnest.

"It will soon be over," they told her.

Nellie lost all sense of time 'til she heard the muf-fled chimes of the clock strike midnight and she cried out in the agony of the final push.

"You have the loveliest baby girl," she heard one of the women say.

"God help the two of them," her mother whispered under her breath.

Nellie Goes to Paris

Nellie Murphy had dreams of a life in Paris. When her daughter Rosie was four months old, she took off for that city and left her baby in the care of her mother, Biddy. She promised she would be back right away to take Rosie to Paris with her, but she didn't show up until four years later. It was the 1920's, the best of all times in Paris. Nellie had met a Frenchman named Belvoir and borne him a couple of children.

When Nellie returned, Biddy refused to give Rosie up—and this started a life of bitterness for everyone concerned. When Rosie was twelve, she was asked in a court of law to choose between her mother and her granny. She chose to live with her granny. It was a very traumatic experience for her. In the end, Nellie had seven children with three different fathers. "Her beauty was her downfall," my mother Rosie always said.

I met Nellie a few times when I was around seven or eight, but never really knew her. She lived in Smithfield, one of the oldest parts of Dublin with cobblestone streets, outdoor fruit and vegetable markets and a fish market that had been there for hundreds of years. All I can recall about her is she was very tall and wore her long black hair in a thick braid wrapped around her head.

The times I visited her, she had a habit of crying and repeating, "Why did Rosie marry that bastard Paddy Jackson?" Then she would complain about him and criticize him. I didn't like her on account of that, because at that time I loved my Daddy. I told Mammy I didn't like the things she said about Daddy and refused to go back to her place after a few visits.

Betty's Baby Boy

Daddy would have been eight months old at the time of my mother Rosie's birth. His mother, Betty Jackson, also had to deal with being a woman alone with a child. This is the story I pieced together years later, with my mother's help...

Betty Jackson, Nellie's dear friend, boarded the mail boat at Dun Laoghaire that would take her to Holyhead. From there, she would go by train to Liverpool. She had not told anyone except Lizzie Kane and Nellie Murphy that she was expecting. Her family thought she was taking a summer job as a laundress at a small, exclusive hotel in Liverpool in exchange for room and board. Her mother and father had been annoyed at her for "stepping out" with an Englishman, and her brothers had chased the two of them from the lane when Betty attempted to bring him home for tea. Her family was Republican and had no time for Britain, its king or its people.

Betty settled in easily enough when she got to Liverpool, but it was a lonely slog away from her friends. She sent letters home to Dublin full of fanciful lies. She'd met a fella, she said, and he wanted to marry her. Later, she said they'd gotten married and she was expecting a baby. Some months later, she stepped off the mail boat in Dun Laoghaire harbor carrying her baby son Patrick in her arms. Her mother, Catherine, was waiting for her. Betty said her husband would follow her to Dublin in a few months, but of course there was never any sign of a husband and nothing more was ever said of it.

It was wartime and in every European port, there were girls left holding fatherless babies. It was just another of the tragedies of war. Some of the fathers died in the war, others never intended to be fathers in the first place.

When Paddy was eight years old, Betty married and started another family without him. She left him with her mother, Catherine. They lived less than half a mile from each other, but she never again recognized him as her son. When Betty died, he found out about it through reading the obituaries. He went to the funeral, but was not invited to sit with the family.

Daddy was abandoned by his father before birth and then dumped by his mother. He had no experience of caring, family, commitment, or responsibility. He was by all reports uncontrollable as a child—drinking, smoking, gambling and running wild in the streets of Dublin. He never recovered from being an eight-year-old boy who was wounded and unloved.

Nellie Murphy's daughter, Rose, and Betty Jackson's son, Patrick, grew up and married each other. Over the years Rosie paid a heavy price for his loveless childhood.

Grace

In my teenage years, I hated being at home and blamed most of the problems on my father. I couldn't stand the constant squabbling, the name-calling and the flying objects. I carried those memories around with me, even after I got married and moved to America. What I had buried deep inside me was how much my father and I had adored each other when I was a child.

Decades later in San Francisco, I began doing Family Reconstruction psychodrama in a group of twelve people. For a whole year, we examined the family history of each person in the group, one by one; we played out the different characters. When it was my turn the other eleven people in the group played members of my family. Slowly, in that process, I began moving toward wanting to forgive my father and to reconcile with him. I realized that, although I had been really angry at him, I could never hate him.

Before I could forgive my father, I had to *want* to forgive him. Before I could want to forgive him, I had to learn about his life. He rarely talked about himself, except in joking ways, but I pieced together his story with my mother's help and began reaching out to Daddy in ways that he could accept. I started making more phone calls home. If he answered the phone, I would engage him in conversation instead of asking for my mother immediately. Sometimes our talk was just banter; other times, I would ask him little things about his life. Slowly, we began dipping into the well of love that we had shared when I was a small child.

I resolved to go to Ireland and try to make my peace with him. I didn't want to read him a litany of complaints; it was more important just to heal the wounds and be connected with him.

I was nervous when I got to Ireland and didn't know if I could go ahead with the plan. As luck would have it, I got up early one morning to find my father in an armchair studying the racing form. My mother was still asleep upstairs.

"May I talk to you?" I asked, and sat down on the floor at his feet.

"What's up?" he replied, putting his head close to mine.

"I just want to tell you that I love you." I couldn't say it without crying. "I'm sorry for any pain I might have caused you."

He hugged me and he began to cry, too, as he stroked my head. "I've always loved you," he said.

We sat like that, crying and holding each other. In a million years, I could not have imagined the bliss I felt in those five or ten minutes.

On the day I was flying home out of Shannon Airport, I called my parents in Dublin to say goodbye. My mother answered the phone and said, "Have you seen your father? He hitchhiked from here at five o'clock this morning."

That's when I spotted him running through the terminal. He threw his arms around me, crying. "I just had to see you one more time to tell you how much I love you. I'm afraid I'll die without seeing you again," he said.

As far as anyone knows, my father was not ill when we hugged at Shannon Airport—but I never saw him alive again.

To Wake a Father

୰

One Saturday morning about six months after my father and I made our peace, he asked Mammy if she'd like to go into town. "I'd like to buy you something for your birthday and we can go see Richard Harris in that new film *The Field*."

"What's seldom is wonderful," she replied, and began looking through her wardrobe for something nice to wear. They rode the crowded bus down Thomas Street. As it passed St. John's Lane Church my father leapt out of his seat and said he wanted to go to Confession. This surprised Mammy because for the most part the two of them only went to Mass and Confession because the neighbors might gossip if they didn't.

"You're getting very religious in your old age," my mother needled him. After Confession, he said he would rather go for a pint than go to the movies.

"I'll get you a surprise for your birthday," he told her when she left him at the door of the pub. That night when he got home, he told her, "Don't bother steeping the corned beef for tomorrow's dinner; I'm going to die tonight."

"You were well enough to swill down the Arthur Guinness all day, you auld hypochondriac," she said, and waited for the retort that never came. He went to bed and she brought him a cup of tea. As she tucked him in, she saw that he was sweating and shivering at the same time.

"I'm telling ye Rosie, I'm going. I'm sorry I gave you such a hard life. Tell all the kids I love them and the grandkids, too." He started to wheeze and rattle, and panic took hold of my mother. Just then, the front door opened and Patrick, the youngest, ran up the stairs and said he'd been at a club and had had a terrible premonition. The six-foot-five son picked up the old man like a rag doll and carried him downstairs to where the last embers were fading in the hearth.

"Virgin Mary, take me," were my father's last words. He was dead when the ambulance arrived.

By the time my daughter, Aisling, and I arrived in Dublin from San Francisco, my father was already "laid out" and was being "waked." The place was filled with laughing and talking and drinking. Tall tales were being told and tears being shed. He just lay there in the coffin as if he were sleeping off a few pints. It was Halloween and outside, rubber tires were being set ablaze and there were Draculas, werewolves, ghosts, goblins, witches, fairies and leprechauns abroad.

When it was time for the body to be taken to the nearby church, the men came and maneuvered the coffin down the narrow staircase. As the family and friends followed the hearse on foot, some kids with sooty faces ran alongside, beating out a rhythm on some dustbin lids. The moon was almost full and bonfires were blazing. As we passed one of the neighbors' houses, the curtains were slowly drawn back and two hairy monsters appeared. We all started howling with laughter, and I thought of how my father could make everybody laugh, especially in sad situations. It was his attempt at relieving their pain.

After leaving the coffin at the church, we adjourned to the local pub to continue the wake and sang every song ever written. At closing time, we sauntered home in small groups, my mother surrounded by her children and grandchildren. As the church bell tolled midnight, it struck us that it was the first of November, our mother's birthday. We all sang, "Happy birthday to you, Happy birthday to you..."

"Your father said he was going to surprise me for my birthday," she said, and we cried and laughed all at once.

At the funeral Mass the next day, the parish priest mentioned that his father had known my father when they were both young men. He told a story I hadn't heard before. My father had won a singing contest at the Theatre Royal in Dublin when he was in his twenties, and was booked for a week of recitals. On opening night, he arrived at the theatre so drunk he couldn't perform. The popular story, according to the parish priest, was that my father fell into the orchestra pit. That was the end of his career, except for the unpaid sessions, dinner dances and hooleys.

I treasure the memory of my father singing, and often dream of him. In one recent dream, he was giving an operatic recital—and he was singing in fluent Italian.

Occasionally I work with the San Francisco Opera as a "super," a non-singing walk-on part. One time, I was chosen to stand on a pedestal modeling a costume designed by David Hockney for the opening night extravaganza of Puccini's *Turandot*. When the tenor sings "Nessun Dorma," one of opera's best loved arias, I always imagine I can hear my dad singing along in impeccable Italian.

A Twist of Fate

∾

My father's last act before he died was to hand my brother Patrick a pawn ticket and apologize that it was all he had to leave anyone. Had he given us enough warning, like another hundred years or so, we might have had enough money put away to pay his funeral expenses. My mother had been making regular payments for thirty years to "the society man," who came to her door every Friday night, rain or shine, to collect for the insurance policy. Over those thirty years, the sixpences grew into shillings, then graduated to half-crowns and then to pound notes—but there was still not enough money on the policy to bury the Da.

We sorted that out. Someone knew someone who knew someone who could get a discount. The people on the street where we lived took up a collection to supplement the money from the insurance policy. Ad-hoc fundraisers are always something you can depend on with the Irish.

Daddy was buried on All Souls Day and was given the best send-off party that anyone ever saw, courtesy of the pub where he had spent all his money. When he was finally laid in the ground, it occurred to us that we didn't have a headstone for the grave. Nor did we have the money to get one.

Patrick had the bright idea of making a simple wooden cross out of the headboard from our father's bed. The grave was bare for a couple of months while Patrick whittled and keened. Eventually the cross went up, but within no time someone had dumped it in the trash container amongst the dead flowers. Simplicity wasn't appreciated in this graveyard.

When my husband heard this tale of woe, he offered to start a fund for the headstone and chipped in a couple of hundred dollars. My brother Sean matched that amount and before we knew it, we had enough money to put a marker on the grave. Sean and I went to a quarry in Connemara because we wanted a Celtic cross made from the beautiful rich green Connemara marble. The price of the marble surprised us. We ordered a smaller cross, in a paler shade of green, than we had planned. Next, we had to get the cross across Ireland from Galway to the graveyard in Dublin, a distance of ninety miles. We asked some friends in Galway to take it in their truck, but when we got back to Dublin the keepers of the graveyard refused to accept the cross. It wasn't purchased from them and did not meet their specifications. The cross was supposed to have a concrete base with very specific dimensions.

The lads with the pickup truck had to go back to Galway and had no choice but to deliver the headstone to my mother's living room, which was only a few blocks from the graveyard. "Yiz better cover it up," my mother told them. "I don't think I want to be looking at that blank spot they've left for my name when me time comes, God help me." So the Celtic cross with our father's name and the epitaph "No Better Man" (his favorite description of himself) was left in the living room. The funds had all dried up.

In a strange case of "wonders never cease," my handsome, debonair brother Patrick began dating one of the heirs to the Guinness fortune. Before flying off for a weekend in Barbados, he thought he should bring the lady home to meet his mother. The heiress had only a limited knowledge of working-class Irish culture and was unfamiliar with any custom involving headstones in the living room. When the yarn was unraveled she took out her checkbook and wrote a big one to cover the costs of installing the cross at the graveyard.

It was a popularly held belief that our father was conceived on Guinness, weaned on Guinness, and in the end he was saved from the disgrace of an unmarked grave by Guinness. And in the bargain, he got back some of the money he had squandered over the decades on that thick black brew.

Time Makes Us Kinder

೪

One day not long ago, my mother was very much on my mind. I knew why. I was scrubbing the kitchen floor on my hands and knees because the squeegee mop had fallen apart.

I was sweating and angry and aching as I pushed the scrubbing brush back and forth over the ancient linoleum. It made me think of all the times my mother went down on her hands and knees to scrub floors, other people's floors. As often as not she was pregnant. She did it to feed her children. I was doing it because of a broken mop that could be replaced. When I realized that, I immediately got over my resentment. I shifted my attitude and gladly, willingly scrubbed the floor.

During my many visits home to Ireland over the years, I've tried to spoil my mother as much as I can. Once I gave her a beautiful beaver-lamb coat that actress Ruth Gordon had given to me. It gave me great pleasure to give Mammy a wonderful coat that had belonged to a famous person. Besides, Ruth was much closer to my mother's 5'2 than to my 5'9.

My favorite ways of spoiling my mother don't necessarily involve material things, although she has never lost her love of clothes and style. One of the ways I treat her is to give her foot massages. Her feet and legs get swollen easily and, with all the pregnancies, she has had more than her share of varicose veins. I have found it to be a humbling experience to sit on the floor before my mother and massage peppermint lotion into her feet and rosemary oil on her legs. If she needs her corns pared, I do that as well.

As I sit at her feet, any misunderstandings we've had in the past seem to wash away. A constant flow of compassion and forgiveness passes back and forth between us. We can be two ordinary women, or we can be mother and daughter, or I can be the mother and she can be the daughter. It is not a spoken exchange. There is no analysis or judgment. It just *is*.

Sometimes we might start singing a song in Irish together and become two little giggly girls singing "*Baidin Fheilimi*" or "*Eamonn an Chnoic*," struggling to remember the words or to do some harmonizing.

Each person shows love in a different way, and I am always on the lookout for signs of love. My mother has her own unique way of expressing hers. While I am home, we may go to a play together and perhaps to the Shelbourne Hotel for afternoon tea. She will insist that it is too expensive and say, "You shouldn't waste your hard-earned money." The next day, she will tell the neighbors that she saw such and such a body from *Dail Eireann*, the Irish Government, or perhaps some television personality.

The neighbors will say, "There goes Rosie, bragging again."

If they pass the remark to her face, she will respond by saying, "Sure haven't I plenty to brag about?"

Everyone's an Expert

≈

I read an ad in the newspaper that couriers were needed to carry computer chips from San Francisco to the Intel plant in Dublin, and signed on immediately. That allowed me to make countless trips to Ireland every year for a few years, all *gratis*.

I'd get a call from Paul Downey at Celtic Travel around ten or eleven o'clock in the morning, asking me if I could be on the next plane out to Dublin. I always said yes. I might be at work, but would just get up from my desk and announce, "Sorry, I have to go to Ireland." And off I'd go.

On one of my visits, I found my mother in very poor health. "She is just acting sick for your benefit," said my sister. "She doesn't want you to go out West without her."

"She's making herself sick because she wants your full and undivided attention," said my brother.

I couldn't accept that my mother's condition was psychosomatic, and I said so.

"We see her all the time," they countered. "We're around her more often than you are. You only see her once a year. There's nothing wrong with her that she hasn't brought on herself."

Anyone with eyes could see that our mother wasn't well. She was bloated and spotty.

"Who's your doctor now?" I asked her. "I'll phone him."

"I'm still seeing Dr. Mack," she replied.

I couldn't believe my ears. Could this be the same doctor my father had cursed with his every breath? She had reported him to the medical board at least once in relation to my father's health care, and at least once in relation to her own. My father used to say that Dr. Mack must have gotten his license in a Lucky Dip or a Christmas Cracker.

"Oh, no," my mother told me. "This is not old Dr. Mack. It's young Dr. Mack, his son."

"The one they say is a morphine addict?" I asked.

My mother is from the old school that teaches you to completely trust, bend the knee or tip the forelock to any male person in authority. I believe this is a condition set deep in the very cells of all people who have been oppressed over the centuries. In Ireland there was the Crown, then the rent collector, the landlord, the priest and more recently the doctor to obey. So my mother went along with whatever the doctors said. On young Dr. Mack's advice, she was taking one pill for water retention, another to prevent blood clots and a third for the arthritis in her knees. At the same time, she prided herself on not being zombified by Valium like many of her neighbors.

We phoned the doctor, and he came to the house. He said the different pills she had been taking had clashed, hence the fiery rash. He brushed over the fact that he was the one who had prescribed all of those "clashing" pills, and gave her another "little pill" to set things right. She listened to my input about a homeopathic remedy and then went ahead and took the pill.

I went out to County Clare for a few days and tried not to feel guilty about leaving her as I sat eating lobster and brown bread washed down with Guinness at Linnane's overlooking the Flaggy Shore. When I got back to Dublin, she had been hospitalized. The toxicity of the drugs had compromised her immune system. There was no diagnosis, no name for what was happening to her. I tried to talk to her about fear and life and death, but she changed the subject by saying, "Can you believe that monstrosity that's being built right next door to the hospital?" So I just sat with her. There were a couple of times when I thought she was getting ready to give up the ghost.

Back home that night, the Greek chorus resumed.

"She's got a good twenty years left in her," said my niece of my seventy-nine-year-old mother.

"She really just needs a vacation in the sun, Portugal or somewhere like that," chimed in my brother.

"Some money in the bank would really help her," said my sister.

"Am I losing my grip on reality?" I asked myself as I watched this theatre of the absurd unfold. The more I expressed what I was seeing and feeling, the more hostile and angry the rest of the family became. At night I dreamt of being stoned to death as I struggled to crack the code of why I was experiencing one thing and everyone else was experiencing something entirely different.

Returning to San Francisco was difficult, as my mother continued to go in and out of hospital and the mysterious rash waned and then flared up again with the accompanying organ dysfunction. I started keeping a picture of my mother in the very front of my mind. She was happy and healthy, sitting in a garden all bathed in light. She was wearing a blue dress and hat and smelling of roses, the flower for which she was named.

Darling Mother

ও

"I've bought tickets for Bruce Springsteen" my husband told me over the phone to lure me back from Dublin to San Francisco. But I had no immediate plans to return. I was in mourning: my mother had died two weeks earlier.

I'd gotten on the next plane to Dublin when my brother Patrick called to tell me the end was near. At the hospital she'd been loosely diagnosed with kidney failure and given five days to live. She wanted to die at home, so we made a comfortable place for her downstairs in the front parlor and divided up the work. Gemma was the cook, because she is a great chef. Kala's forte was cleaning, I was the caregiver/doctor/nurse and Patrick was in charge of all ingoing and outgoing phone calls.

Our mother accepted that she was dying and said she was ready. For days, she held court and reminisced about her life. She sang songs and told stories and described some of the marvelous clothes she had worn in her heyday. She had a captive audience, because we never left her side. We nursed her twenty-four hours a day and she adored having most of her children and some of her grandchildren around her.

The five days she was given to live turned into twenty-eight days—and she was very unhappy about that. Everything was working well except her kidneys. Her brain was as fiercely bright as it had always been. For four weeks, she was hardly able to eat or drink anything. Nothing stayed down, but still she prevailed.

When the weather was warm enough, we'd wrap her in a blanket and she'd sit in a wheelchair in her back

garden amongst the lavender and petunias. We sat out-
doors the night of a full moon and lit tall candles at twilight and sang every song we could think of with the
word "moon" in it. She had her sense of humor until the
end. One day she said to me, "God forgive me but I'm
enjoying this global warming. I suppose they'll be growing bananas in County Kerry after I'm gone."

Music was one of her greatest joys. "As long as I
have my music I'll be fine," she said constantly. During
her last days she got sustenance from Jussi Bjorling, her
favorite tenor, and also from Mario Lanza, Ennio Morri-
cone and Donegal fiddler Eugene O'Donnell.

The weeks wore on. Friends and neighbors came by
to visit, and my good friend Josephine frequently
brought delicious food to share. Rosie's dear friend
Maureen came by and held her hand, and together they
sang a couple of tunes. They'd sung in a choir together
for thirty-three years. Maureen said, "Rosie, you'll be at
the pearly gates ahead of me so keep an eye out for me,
won't you."

Another of her friends said to her one day. "Ah sure
you'll be back on your feet again in no time."

My mother replied, "Indeed I won't be back on my
feet. I'll slip away quietly one of these nights in my
sleep."

But it was not to be. After two weeks, she began to
fail. Too weak to talk much or to sing, she tried to force
herself to die but couldn't. She fought with God and was
in a power struggle with Him. "Why won't He take me?"
she asked.

I sat up with her overnight every night. I stroked
her head and held her hands and talked to her about
letting go. I told her it was time to surrender. She said,
"But I can't." And so she suffered on. I felt tremendous
sadness that a woman whose life had been as hard as my

mother's should also have a hard death. It seemed unfair.

Before she lost consciousness for the last time, she looked up at me with her almost transparent blue eyes. "Is that my Renée?" she asked and held her arms out to me. The boundary lines of who was mother and who was child disintegrated as we held onto each other for dear life.

Nat King Cole was singing "Unforgettable" when she drew her last breath.

When we'd had a good screaming, weeping and collapsing session, Kala and I washed her and laid her out. It was the first time we'd seen her naked. She was beautiful, like a girl, with her fine lightly freckled skin spread tightly over her high cheekbones. Then Patrick washed and set her hair and a mortician came by the house and embalmed her. We dressed her in a favorite blue dress, per her instructions, and earrings to match. She looked serene and peaceful. For a couple of days people came by to sit with her until it was time to take her body to the church. One of her friends said, "I'll spend the night in the church with her so she won't be lonely."

The next day at Mass I sang "The Rose" as a tribute to my darling mother, and Kala delivered a eulogy. Then we laid her in the ground and that was the hardest part of all.

So I came back to San Francisco and I went to hear Bruce Springsteen, but my heart wasn't in it. You only lose your mother once and I'm wondering will I ever get over the loss of mine.

Part 2
Early Years

≈

My parents had an enormous impact on my early years, but they were not the only influence. As I began to move into the world outside our home, I learned things they couldn't have taught me.

Illusions

✌

Mary Comerford was in my class at school in Dublin. When we were nine, Mary received a pair of red and gold brocade shoes from an aunt who had emigrated to Buffalo, New York. The shoes had upturned toes, just like those in the storybooks of *1001 Arabian Nights*. I was dazzled by them and I formed an image of Buffalo, New York, that was as exotic as any place in Persia. I was jealous over the shoes and also envious because Mary had an aunt, when I myself had no aunts, uncles or grandparents in my life.

Like many people and events in my childhood, those shoes sowed the seed for a later adventure. Many years and many pairs of shoes later, I took the Canadian government up on their offer of a $100 loan for passage to that country. I was twenty-one when I left Dublin and sailed to Montreal in search of work. I had only $60 to my name, but I knew the first thing I wanted to do when I got there was to cross the border and visit Buffalo, New York.

The bus trip was long and harrowing. Immigration officials at the border even took me off the bus when they learned I didn't have enough money for a weekend in Buffalo. The delay agitated my fellow bus passengers and, either for that reason or because I convinced them I had no intention of staying in the U.S. illegally and only wanted to view the city of Buffalo, they eventually let me cross.

As the bus pulled in to the downtown station, I'd already seen enough to know that all my dreams of Buffalo had been illusion. There was litter everywhere and graffiti on every surface, even on the trunks of trees. Trees had grown into overhead electrical wires, bicycles lay broken on the pavement, and smashed-up cars and old refrigerators littered the streets. I wept when I found the place more like the pictures of bombed-out London than like the Hanging Gardens of Babylon.

And it had all started with Mary Comerford's red and gold brocade shoes. Around the time of those shoes, I was spending a lot of evenings at the Comerfords' house. I loved it and thought they were posh because they lived in the row of Georgian houses and I lived in the tenements in the lane. I was learning the violin in school at the time, but didn't own one so Mary Comerford's brother let me practice on his when I'd go around after school. I mastered "Three Blind Mice" and "Twinkle Twinkle Little Star."

If I stayed at the Comerfords' house late, Mary's father would take me home on the crossbar of his bicycle. One night he forced a kiss on me and stuck his tongue in my mouth. I was only nine years old! I never went back to their house again. I gave up the violin and never told a soul the reason why.

Something else happened around the time of "the kiss." Mary and I were playing in the lane when my father appeared carrying what we decided was a dead body wrapped in a black coat. He pushed his way past us, went into the rooms where we lived and shut the door behind him.

Mary and I were frightened. We tried to guess whose body was in the black coat. I said it was Bleeder Lawlor, who sold newspapers on the corner. We peeped through the keyhole to find out who the dead person was, and that's when I saw it—a full carcass of beef, all prepared and ready for the butcher's shop.

My mother screamed at my father, "What about the poor man who lost this? He'll be in terrible trouble and it'll probably be taken out of his wages." She told my father that, even though we were often hungry, she would not stoop to this. My father said he hadn't stolen it, that he was coming home down Mount Street when the beef fell off the back of a lorry and he saw his opportunity. He went out into the street, covered up the meat with his overcoat and threw it over his shoulder. (For many years after that, I thought the expression "It fell off the back of a lorry" started with Daddy and the meat carcass.)

I was never told the details, but the next day a man came to our place to claim the meat. He gave my mother rashers and sausages, liver and kidneys. He gave my father a few bob for his honesty and of course my da went straight away to The Hive pub at the end of our street. He staggered home blind drunk later that night singing, "We are poor little lambs who have lost our way, Baa baa baa. We are little black sheep who have gone astray, Baa baa baa." He always sang that when he was very, very drunk.

I felt mortally ashamed in front of Mary Comerford. On top of that, I was still feeling sick from the incident with her father. All of it forced me to quit my friendship with her.

So when the twenty-one-year-old me stood weeping in the streets of Buffalo, New York, I was also my nine-year-old self weeping for the loss of my darling friend Mary Comerford, and the violin lessons, and for my father whom I'd shut out of my heart because I couldn't take the pain. I also wept because back when I was nine years old, I'd had no one to tell what was going on inside of me. I knew if I told anyone, they would say, "It's all your own fault.

Uncertainties

ॐ

Christmas is coming; the goose is getting fat.
Please put a penny in the old man's hat.
If you haven't got a penny a halfpenny will do.
If you haven't got a halfpenny a farthing will do.
If you haven't got a farthing, then God bless you!

I remember jumping rope and chanting that rhyme in the weeks leading up to Christmas. I don't remember every detail of every Christmas, but I do remember it was always bitterly cold and every penny we had was spent on coal. The main focus of our household, aside from food, was having a fire in the grate.

We often depended on the kindness of strangers to help put a meal on the table on Christmas Day. It was not unusual for publicans and shopkeepers to make gifts of food to their faithful customers, whether or not those customers owed them money. We usually got a pound of butter or sugar, and maybe a few pounds of flour, from Mrs. Bannon in the shop next door. Another shopkeeper might give us a fat red candle to burn in the window all night, or a marzipan cake or plum pudding. Sometimes our neighbor Mr. Daly, who sold coal, would get carried away by the spirit of the season and give us a sack of coal in a fit of generosity. And the St. Vincent De Paul would come around our lane and give families vouchers to trade for clothes or shoes.

When I no longer believed in Santa Claus, my mother and I would go to Woolworth's on Grafton Street and buy several tiny naked dolls, about four inches high with moveable arms and legs. We'd sit up late on Christmas Eve in front of the fire to knit and sew minute outfits for them. We put them in the younger ones' stockings and pretended they were from Santa. Then we'd hang paper chains from the ceiling, fastened with a large paper star at the center. Sprigs of holly were tucked behind the mirror above the fireplace. We never had a Christmas tree.

Besides the tiny dolls, we might get Dandy and Beano, The Boy's Own, the Four Marys annuals and some comic books. We'd hang socks on the mantelpiece, and into them would go small gifts like a harmonica, a Cadbury's selection box and maybe a monkey-on-a-stick. Bigger gifts, if there were any, were left at the foot of the bed. Toy musical instruments were popular—paper concertinas, pennywhistles, drums and xylophones.

Most of the children were happy with anything they got. On Christmas morning, all the kids in our lane would come out to show off their toys and books and sometimes swap or barter the presents that didn't totally delight them. Meanwhile, the mammies were cooking—if they had anything to cook—and the daddies were on their way home from the pub, with just enough time to see the bird being taken out of the oven. Robbie Robinson, our neighbor in the tenement, would be anxiously inquiring if we were having turkey. He would ask my mother to save the leftover carcass and then would spend the next several months or years polishing and decorating it until he turned it into a beautiful Spanish galleon, complete with sails.

I never expected much at Christmas. If we had any money for toys, it was spent on the younger kids. I'd get a Cadbury's selection box if I was lucky. I never got a doll.

When I was in my thirties, I decided to have the kind of Christmas I'd dreamed of as a child, but never experienced. If I wanted a doll, the solution was easy. I just bought myself a doll. I wrapped it up beautifully with a card that said, "To Renée from Santa." Having a Christmas tree was part of the new habit I was creating, and I put my toys and gifts under the tree. Some of the parcels said, "To Renée from Renée." I knitted Christmas stockings to hang by the chimney and crocheted dozens of snowflakes, dipped them in sugar water and spent days experimenting with making them stiff by baking them in the oven. When they cooled off, I glued on scads of tiny crystal beads to make them sparkle. I even bought a crèche and several angels.

Now when I get up on Christmas morning, I light the fire and make a cup of tea. I take the liver from the goose I will cook later in the day, fry it in butter and have it on a piece of toast. If I really want to go overboard, I'll have the goose liver with a glass of champagne. My husband, daughter, grandchildren and I sit by the fire and open our presents. We generally give each other books and music with maybe a doll, a swan or an elephant figurine for me. When I open the presents from me to me, I act surprised and feel full of joy.

I never venture out on Christmas Day. My friends Paula and Ken Minkus come around eleven and bring champagne. I put out the pâté and smoked salmon and a few other goodies. They visit for a couple of hours and then go on their merry way to celebrate with their own kids and grandkids. I let the joy of Christmas wash over me. What matters the most is I have a roof over my head, a fire in the hearth, loving friends and family and plenty of food to eat.

"The Models" Together Again

≈

My sister Gemma came from Ireland to visit me in San Francisco in 2007 and was constantly bemoaning the weight she'd put on. "Welcome to the real world," I told her. To cheer us up I went looking through a stash of old photographs for one taken when we were young and svelte and gorgeous. I found it! We were at the Dublin Horse Show in Ballsbridge. We looked very glamorous in our fancy hats tilted just so and our chic dresses with not an ounce of fat in sight. We recalled how we'd been known in our old neighborhood as "the models."

I was about eight when Gemma was born, and some dramatic changes happened in our household around that time.

Mammy credited Gemma's birth with Daddy's change in attitude towards work. He actually went looking, and eventually got a steady job as an ambulance driver at Cherry Orchard Hospital. Daddy adored Gemma, maybe because she most resembled Mammy, and she was crazy about him in return. I didn't feel any jealously or resentment; I'd already gone sour on him.

Riffling through those drawers full of pictures during Gemma's visit, I came upon one that brought back a flood of memories. The picture shows me, my brother Sean, two younger sisters Fiona and Kala and my good friend, Kathleen Kelly. Kathleen was the postman's daughter and lived in our lane. Her family was better off than ours; she is the only one with a bathing suit that fits.

(The Kellys were some of the first people in Dublin to own a TV set, even though at the time Ireland did not yet have a TV network of its own. All the kids in our lane would gather when it was dark and stand on tiptoes outside the Kellys' front window, trying to get a glimpse of the television. All we ever saw were lights flashing on and off.)

That photo of us kids in bathing suits was taken at Sandymount Strand when I was about ten. I'm looking directly into the camera. I have short blonde hair and eyes as big as saucers. I'm wearing a grownup's bathing suit with the straps tied in a knot at the back of my neck so that the front comes all the way up to my chin. The elastic in the swimsuit is stretched and saggy from age. I remember being embarrassed at having to wear it.

We often walked from Verschoyle Place to that particular spot on Sandymount Strand. It was about a mile, and then a little further to Merrion Gate. My mother would push a big pram that held the current baby and usually a toddler or two. I remember vividly the day that photo was taken because baby Gemma, who was barely walking at the time, disappeared into thin air. My mother was wailing and all the kids were hushed and frightened —as if we were to blame for Gemma's disappearance.

I don't know where my father was. He was probably digging for cockles, because we often had a couple of bucketfuls to take home with us for dinner. If we were lucky our treat at the end of the day was a hot loaf of Boland's bread and steamed clams with salt and vinegar.

Everybody at the strand that day headed out to look for Gemma. In Ireland the summer days are light until past ten o'clock at night, so we had no fears about the dark. She was eventually found right at the water's edge. Fortunately, the sea was not wild there. There were no dangerous currents, just a gentle lapping when the tide was in. Because she had not yet learned to speak, she couldn't explain what had happened.

Decades later, in my kitchen, Gemma and I thought about those days we loved at Sandymount Strand and Merrion Gate—and the times when, if Mammy had a few extra bob, she would take us on the train to Killiney for a real treat.

I asked Gemma if she recalled anything from the day she went missing. She said she remembered an older girl holding her head underneath the water as if to drown her—but she refused to disclose the name.

In May, 2011, for old time's sake Gemma and I went to Sandymount Strand. She brought a primus stove, a kettle and the makings of tea. We sat in the cold and drizzle and had hot tea and coconut macaroons. We had a great time.

An Involuntary Move

❦

I was eleven when we were evicted from our two rooms in Verschoyle Place for not paying the weekly rent of six shillings and sixpence. The Sheriff came and put us and our few possessions out on the street.

Robert Briscoe was the Lord Mayor of Dublin at the time and the Mansion House, his residence, was about half a mile from where we lived. My brother Sean and I went down to Kildare Street and asked to see the Lord Mayor. I don't remember who we actually saw, but we told our story and between that and someone Daddy knew at *Clann na Pobhlachta*, the Irish Republican Party, by day's end we had a corporation/council house in Ballyfermot, a part of the city that was known as Hell's Half Acre.

I remember the overwhelming feelings of shame when we moved our few bits and pieces of furniture using the horse and cart that our neighbor, Mr. Daly, normally used for delivering coal. Our new neighbors in Hell's Half Acre came out to watch us move into number eight. Later that day, kids on the street taunted us, which made the shame even greater.

We had two beds and a couple of chairs, some dishes and our clothes. Once we had everything inside, we kids took to running up and down the stairs. We'd never had stairs before. The house had built-in closets and it wasn't long before we broke them down and chopped them up for firewood. We also had the novelty of a front garden and a large back yard.

The morning after we moved in, Sean and I left the house to find a bus that would take us into town. He had to get to the Christian Brothers' school in Westland Row. I had to get to Loreto Convent at Stephen's Green. We got lost amongst the thousands of houses that all looked alike and wandered aimlessly all day long. Neither of us ever made it to school.

Since there was no money for bus fare anyway, I went to work in a garment factory in Chapelizod to learn pattern making and cutting. I was only twelve, but I looked older.

A Nun to the Rescue

One Sunday after I'd left school and been at the garment factory for a couple of weeks, a stranger came to our door with a message from my teacher, Mother Consolata. My mother and the stranger went into the front room, and the door was shut behind them. I couldn't hear the conversation, but the next day I had bus fare to get to school in the center of the city.

When I got there, Mother Consolata pulled me aside conspiratorially and showed me the hiding place for the bus tickets that she was going to provide for me from that point on. They would be tucked away in the back of one of her desk drawers. She told me she was going to make sure that I had something hot to eat at lunchtime each day as well. It turned out to be a cup of Oxo with two slices of bread and margarine, but I didn't complain. Mother Consolata said it would be "our secret" and I know now that she was trying to protect me from shame.

Shame is poverty's twin. For the next two years, I was privileged to have the best possible education, including free vocal coaching and violin lessons, courtesy of Mother Consolata. I also entered and won a scholarship to a teachers' training college, thanks to her encouragement.

Why she showed such kindness to me is still a mystery, because she was quite abusive to everyone else. None of the kids in my class knew why she was so angry all the time or why the littlest things could set her off. I remember daydreaming one afternoon at my little desk towards the back of the classroom when suddenly I heard her skirts rustling and her bamboo rod swooshing in the air. My heart was pounding as she ran towards me and, luckily for me, ran past and grabbed Kathleen Ryan by the hair. She dragged Kathleen to the front of the classroom and forced her to her knees before the larger than life statue of the Virgin Mary.

Kathleen had forged her mother's name on a sick note and been found out in the lie. The nun took a bottle of holy water from Lourdes and poured the contents over the "liar's" head, at the same time whipping her with the bamboo cane. "Get the devil out of you," she repeated over and over as the whole class sat transfixed in horror.

Mother Consolata continued to beat up on the other kids and even went as far as hitting Mary O'Brien on the side of the head with the fiddle because she was massacring "Three Blind Mice."

Whatever light this dark nun had, she shone on me. I left that school when I was fourteen and that was the last I saw of her.

Get Thee to a Nunnery

೪

In the olden and not-so-olden days, every young Catholic girl in Ireland was expected at least to consider becoming a nun.

"You'd make a great nun, Renée," or "You have a nun's face, Renée," were mantras the Mothers Consolata and Clemency chanted to me at every opportunity. At the same time, I had a coterie of admirers amongst the mothers of my schoolmates who convened in St. Stephen's Green every day, waiting to pick up their children after school. They said I had the makings of an actress.

"You look just like that actress from the play, 'The Bad Seed,'" they told me. I wondered what it meant to be a bad seed and hoped I wasn't one. That comparison with "the bad seed" had a lasting effect on me. I think we forget, as adults, how impressionable and guileless young children are. I was particularly naïve because I didn't have older brothers or sisters to answer my questions or to confide in. I was on my own.

Like most homes in Ireland, we had pictures on the wall of the wounded Jesus with an arrow piercing his bleeding heart and the Virgin Mary with her foot crushing the head of a serpent. We also had a picture of Our Lady of Knock, all dressed up in a Grecian toga-like dress and looking like a Hollywood film star with gold ringlets and rosy cheeks.

I didn't feel right talking to those pictures about my confusion, and instead made up stories and dramas of terrible things happening to me so I could come crying to Mammy. I really just wanted her comfort and to get my questions answered about the real world and "the facts of life." To that end, I once told her that a man had followed me to school and tried to drag me down a laneway near the little church by Merrion Square, but I had screamed and kicked and gotten away. (Strangely, I never said a word when ugly things really did happen to me, like the time when I was seven and an older boy pulled out his penis and said he'd give me a penny if I'd touch it.) I never got the information I wanted. I think she may have been even more uncomfortable with "the facts of life" than I was, despite having all those children.

The question of the nunnery was always before us. I'd see nuns all the time on the streets of Dublin, always in groups or pairs. There were lots of orders—the Sisters of Mercy, the Loreto Nuns, the French Sisters, the Sisters of Charity and the Poor Clares. The Poor Clares were sworn to a vow of silence. I would look at myself in the mirror and imagine being locked up with women all dressed in black, forever rattling their rosary beads and saying their prayers. I'd cry my eyes out at the thought of never seeing Mammy and Daddy again. I would take my imagined drama even further and picture myself being sent off to Africa to help convert "the heathens" and never seeing Ireland again.

As luck would have it, I got to be in several plays about that same time, including a part in "The Bishop's Candlesticks" at the Damer Hall. I experimented more with the actress in me during school holidays, and took to theatrics like a fish to water. I think maybe the nuns saw it coming, my slow fade from the nunnery to the stage. They talked to me about making a pilgrimage to Knock in County Mayo to talk to Our Lady. The Virgin Mary is reported to have appeared there in 1879. Every Irish person will tell you they've done the pilgrimage to

Knock, just as every American believes he or she was at Woodstock.

I made the pilgrimage to Knock to please the nuns, but they never managed to make a nun of me. The only reason I could think of to become a nun was to get three square meals a day, and that wasn't nearly a good enough reason.

Cabin Hunting

୰

The scholarship to the teacher's training college that Mother Consolata had helped me win never panned out. The only money my parents had to provide was for books and a school uniform, but there wasn't enough even for that and we had nobody to ask for a loan. My family was pretty much alone; we had no relatives to speak of.

I had to swallow my anger and disappointment. I understood the situation and knew my mother was heartbroken that she couldn't provide the money to see me through. I settled for a scholarship to Parnell Square Technical School in Dublin, where I would learn practical things like typing and shorthand that would stand me in good stead in the job market.

I'd been singing and acting for a few years at Loreto, my parochial school, and I continued at Parnell. I became a member of a trio with two other girls from school, Valerie Healy and Eva Drake. By day, we sang traditional Irish songs and listened to classical music. By night, we traded our school uniforms for the latest styles and performed the songs of Roy Orbison and the Everly Brothers in a couple of Dublin dancehalls. We were just fourteen or fifteen, and trying to pass as older—innocents acting as sophisticates. I also won prizes for the school at the *Feis Ceoil*, a national music contest, and at other festivals.

Leo Maguire, the famous singer and composer, heard me sing and offered me free vocal coaching at the Municipal School of Music. Maguire composed more than 100 songs, the most famous being "The Whistling

Gypsy." He also encouraged me to take up the harp, saying that I could earn my living by it. The only harpist I was aware of was an old blind woman who played haunting tunes on Grafton Street. It was hard to think of taking harp lessons without any prospect of ever owning a harp. I was barely getting enough to eat and had a hard time scraping up the bus fare to get to the school in the first place. I didn't last long at the lessons.

I don't think most people realized how poor we were or what our family life was like, because I always put up a good front—but I hated life at home and could never settle into Ballyfermot. I hated the fights, the hunger, and the uncertainties. As I grew older, I spent as little time as possible at home and often paraphrased James Joyce, saying, "I'll do anything within reason, but I won't go home." Joyce, of course, had been in exile in Europe and was referring to Ireland as his home. I was merely staying away from my family.

All my interests, friends and activities were in the center of the city, and I was beginning to travel in different circles. I was meeting artists and writers, actors and intellectuals, and becoming part of the café society at the center of Dublin. Ballyfermot might as well have been on another planet, it was so foreign to me. I rarely went there, even to sleep.

I squatted in derelict buildings some nights, or climbed in through windows in the homes of friends from school. Mammy called this "cabin hunting." If I stayed out much past eleven o'clock, when the last bus left the city center for Ballyfermot, I'd have to walk the five miles home. My father would have just come from the pub and would either lock me out or shout to the whole avenue that I was a whore and a prostitute. He'd open the windows and yell, "I'll tell the neighbors what you are." I had never ever been kissed, except for the awful unwelcome one from Mr. Comerford. Rosie McDonald, a neighbor across the street, often took me in for the night.

My poor mother. I hate to think of what I put her through. She sometimes roamed the streets late at night looking for me. Once I heard her knocking at the door of a flat where I was crashing and I ignored her knocks, pretending there was no one home.

By the time I was sixteen, I'd sprouted up to five feet nine inches and got my photo in the newspapers a lot. Some of the photos were for winning prizes for singing or acting in school events or for storytelling at festivals. Others were because I was tall and had developed a personal style that set me apart from other girls my age. I became known as "the model" in our neighborhood and dreamed of the day when I could leave home and strike out on my own to the faraway places that called to me. Many years later, I was knocking around San Francisco with writer Nuala O'Faolain. We were talking about the old days and she turned to me and said, "Sure you were the glamour girl of Dublin."

Mammy scraped and sacrificed to get me decent-looking clothes. She knew a tailor in Winetavern Street who could copy fashions out of *Vogue* magazine for very little money, and I made some of my own clothes by hand. I got my sense of style from my mother; I had the knack of making anything look good.

Shoes were always the hardest part of my wardrobe. Mammy could sew or knit most of our clothes, but she couldn't make shoes. Except for when I made my First Holy Communion and Confirmation, I was always wearing someone else's shoes and they were always too big, too small or too narrow. Even when I got a new pair of shoes, the experience would be short-lived because they'd be pawned shortly after the special event and I'd never see them again. Sometimes when my feet get tired, I have flashbacks to the agony, shame and embarrassment I suffered at not having the right kind of shoes, or sometimes even any decent shoes at all.

The worst hurt came when I was sixteen and going to Parnell Square Tech. A neighbor, Florrie Fields, had given my mother an old pair of shoes to burn in the fire. (Shoes were sometimes the only fuel we had.) They had pointy toes and stiletto heels, and were black with white polka-dots. Mammy broke off the spindly heels in an attempt to make the shoes flat, and that caused the toes to point straight up in the air. I wore those disastrous-looking shoes to school, because I had no others. Mammy suffered as much as I did the day I cried and said I didn't want to leave the house with such eyesores on my feet. En route to school, I caught up with two favorite girls from my class as they walked along O'Connell Street. They took one look at my feet, sniggered and tittered and then crossed to the other side of the street.

I have no shame about wearing second-hand clothes now. It is all in one's perspective of what is shameful. I enjoy browsing the thrift shops for items that are chic and cheap. I like trying to picture the person who wore the clothes before me and I'm happy in the knowledge I'm not being wasteful in a world where everything is considered disposable.

Unrequited Love

و‍

I never really thought about what I wanted to be when I grew up. I just knew that I needed to get a job and help support my family. At sixteen, I left Parnell Square Tech and got a job at Ardiff's Printers. There I met Sean Spain. He was a compositor in the printing shop upstairs and I was a proofreader in the offices downstairs. I think he was twenty-one.

Every day after work, Sean and I would stand on the street corner and talk for hours on end, sometimes until it was dark. We never thought of food or drink, and parted only after the cold had gotten into our bones. He'd ride off on his bicycle in one direction and I'd catch the bus that went the opposite way. We'd have talked about everything under the sun—art, politics, ideas, books, life, you name it. Sean Spain never asked me on a date, nor did he ever kiss me. Our friendship was all about hanging out on street corners discussing, dissecting and analyzing every subject—or so it seemed.

Sean Spain was the first boy I ever loved. I had a big crush on him and saw my opportunity to move things along when I heard that Loreto Convent, my old school, was having a graduation dress dance at a posh hotel. Dress dances were all the rage at the time, and involved renting tuxedoes, buying ball gowns and generally going into debt.

I asked Sean Spain if he'd accompany me to the dress dance and he accepted. I was over the moon. I got my first pair of high heel shoes and visited a hair salon for the first time. A friend of a friend loaned me an evening dress which, mercifully, fit perfectly. All the women on the avenue where I lived came out to see me off on my big night and to "ooh and aah" about my outfit. Some said I looked like a princess. My heart pounded with excitement at the prospect of seeing "Spainer" in a tuxedo.

Sean picked me up and off we went to the dance. He looked like a movie star with his jet black hair slicked back like a Teddy Boy. He presented me with gardenias, as was the custom. During the whole evening, he never once asked me to dance and barely spoke a word to me. I sat there like a lump on a log as he gazed moony-eyed at Dolores Carruth. She had been a couple of years ahead of me in school. I didn't know her well, but appreciated her beauty from a distance. She was someone I admired and envied for several reasons. She wore her long blonde hair in a single plait that went down past her waist. She played the cello and she was an only child.

I was stunned when a schoolmate told me Sean Spain was madly in love with Dolores. He'd probably just accepted my invitation to the dance so he could get closer to her. I should have known all those conversations about the writings of Plato were an indication of something—a platonic relationship, perhaps. Obviously I was not his confidante, or he would have told me about his unrequited love. My relationship with him did not include speaking about matters of the heart.

Pretty soon after that, I was fired from my proofreading job for falling asleep over the galleys one too many times. I had arrived at work that morning wrecked, after having spent the night trying to sleep in a Volkswagen Bug.

I went to live in Paris the next year, developed other interests and eventually I forgot the pain of Sean Spain. Not long after that, I started to think fondly of him and began a correspondence. We had a couple of pleasant exchanges until I included in a letter a quote from Mark Twain about heaven being a pretty boring place with nothing to do on a Saturday night but play the harp. I received a bitter, judgmental letter back. Sean called me wanton and accused me of being an atheist. I was wounded to the core. I had an older, wiser friend help me compose a letter back to him in which I explained that the piece was satire. I told him I was only trying to stimulate a conversation about heaven and hell and religious beliefs, like we used to do when we hung out on the street corner. I never received a reply. And in all my meanderings through the streets of Dublin over the years, I've never encountered Sean Spain. I heard he married, but not Dolores Carruth.

Part 3
Breaking Free

๛

Even though life at home had become intolerable, my process of breaking free was a long process — fits and starts and long lost interludes. It began while I was still living in Dublin and continued when I moved to Paris, returned to Ireland and eventually journeyed to Canada, England, Australia, the United States, and points beyond. My "breaking free" also involved seven years of wandering in the wilderness, and finding the love of my life.

Americans Make an Appearance

When I was sixteen and graduated from Parnell Square Technical School, I immediately began combing newspapers and magazines for extraordinary-sounding jobs that would provide me with a plane ticket to somewhere. Almost anywhere was fine, as long as it was elsewhere.

I applied as a photographer's assistant on a four-month safari across Africa—but when the advertiser wrote that we would "live closer than man and wife," I declined his offer. I'd never been with a man and I was horrified.

As it turned out, I found a greater adventure right there in Dublin. In the years when I was keeping away from home and spending time in the center of the city, I often stayed at the home of the American painter, Hilaire Hiler. Hiler's daughter DeDe and I had been best friends ever since we'd met at the New Amsterdam Café in Dublin. The Hilers lived in a flat in Rathmines that was filled with beautiful art. In the room where I slept, there were floor-to-ceiling reproductions of "A Sunday on La Grand Jatte" by Seurat and Rousseau's "Snake Charmer," painstakingly copied by Hiler.

During the 1920s, Hiler had managed The Jockey, a nightclub in Paris. (I wondered if my grandmother Nellie had ever gone there during her years in Paris.) He was part of the Montparnasse arts crowd and often played jazz piano and saxophone at the club, which was a famous artist's hangout.

DeDe was seventeen when I met her, and her father was sixty-four. He wasn't too old to try and kiss me, but I laughed at him and said he was a dirty old man. I've never forgotten his response: "Every man you meet, whether he is sixteen or sixty-four, is going to want to kiss you."

Earlier when they were living in Big Sur, Hiler had tried to marry DeDe off to the author Henry Miller, who was donkey's years older than she was. DeDe and I fancied ourselves Beatniks. We hung out with musicians and poets, and dressed in nothing but black. We went to literary gatherings in cafés and bars where she would read poetry and I would sing a few tunes. At one point, we were "discovered" by a flamenco performer who was going to turn us into flamenco dancers. We were both 5'9" and both blonde. Go figure. The scheme didn't last long. My young friend got involved with drugs and her friends turned hostile. After that, it seemed as if she just disappeared off the face of the earth.

It was at one of the Hilers' dinner parties that I met the American actor, William Marshall. He had come to Ireland from Paris, where he was living at the time, to perform in the title role of *Othello*. (Michael MacLiammoir played Iago.) He was a last minute replacement for the Irish actor Anew McMaster, who had taken ill. Harold Hobson, the theatre critic for the *London Sunday Times,* called William "the best Othello of our time."

William and I talked all through dinner and struck up an immediate friendship. For the first time, or so it seemed, someone was interested in what I thought and hoped and dreamed. I felt we had more in common than I had with most other people, and he invited me to the Gaiety Theatre to see him in *Othello*.

It was not just the glamour of the theatre that attracted me to him. Through our long talks, I was also learning about American society and the history of African Americans in the United States. William was from the steel town of Gary, Indiana, the only child in a middle class family whose grandparents had been slaves. He had studied at the Actors Studio in New York and was part of the circle of American actors, writers, musicians who had relocated to Paris because of the Hollywood Blacklist. The Hollywood Ten were men who had been jailed for refusing to sign an oath saying they were not Communists. Years later in San Francisco, I would become a close friend of one of them, Lester Cole.

William turned me on to serious reading and gave me books that left lasting impressions. One of them was *Johnny Got His Gun,* by Dalton Trumbo, a blacklisted writer and one of the Hollywood Ten. That book opened my eyes to the devastating consequences of war and made me an anti-war activist for the rest of my life. It's the story of what goes on in the mind of a limbless man being kept alive in a hospital bed, a virtual vegetable who has just returned from World War I.

When I told William my dreams of seeing the big wide world and longing to see Paris, he said he had a friend who could help me if I ever made it there. We swanned it around Dublin for a short time, getting our pictures in all the papers and having a great time. On his last night in Dublin, he became my first lover. Though I was seventeen and he was thirty-seven, I didn't notice a difference in our age or in the color of our skins.

He returned to Paris and we corresponded. He introduced me by mail to his friend Sylvia Jarrico, the one who could help me if I ever made it to Paris.

Paris, Here I Come

❧

I read in *Variety* magazine that a nightclub in Paris was holding auditions for showgirls. I had been taking a ballet class for fitness and owned a leotard for that purpose, so I had a photographer friend come to the dance studio and take a photo of me posing at the *barre*. I was not really a dancer, but I applied, auditioned and got the job at La Nouvelle Eve. I signed a two-year contract to work in Paris, Las Vegas and Buenos Aires, but had no intention of seeing the contract through to the end. It was just a way to escape my home life and to reunite with my lover in Paris. I was seventeen, and finally getting away from home for good.

I left Dublin on a chilly April day in 1963 with my paltry possessions of one black dress, a pair of red boots and a red chiffon scarf packed in a cardboard suitcase. I had very little else. I brought with me an armload of daffodils from a friend's garden, the only gifts I could afford. I was going to meet Sylvia Jarrico, William Marshall's friend, and she was going to put me up.

(The same week I left, my beloved brother Sean ran away with Fossett's Circus. He couldn't bear life at home without me. Mammy didn't find out where he had gone until she read in the paper that he had tried to bring a baby elephant into a bar in Galway. His job at the circus was helping with the elephants.)

Sylvia lived at 226 Rue du Rivoli, a glorious 16th century building overlooking the Tuileries Gardens. Her apartment had high ceilings and rooms with wall-to-wall books, tapestries and floor-to-ceiling mirrors. I had never met her in person. William had only "introduced" us by letter.

When she opened the door, she was wearing a simple blue dress and no makeup. I thought she was the maid! I could hear William taking a singing lesson in a room nearby, so I knew I must be in the right place. They were very gracious. I gave Sylvia the daffodils, and she served me a platter of oysters with good French bread and a glass of dry vermouth. It was a marvelous beginning, and I took to the lifestyle like a fish to water.

My time in Paris was exciting and full of contradictions. I was happy that there were no class boundaries and no intellectual hierarchy in my new circle of friends. My wit and good looks were appreciated, as were my anecdotes about Ireland. It seemed everyone had a soft spot for the Irish.

William introduced me to Ginette Spanier, who was the Directrice of Pierre Balmain Couture, and I went to see her and meet Monsieur Balmain. I'd done some hair and make-up modeling at Fernand Aubry on the Rue de la Boetie and went there en route to Balmain to get dolled up. I wore a Rodier suit and jewelry borrowed from Sylvia. The *chef de cabine* brought me in to meet some of the other models who were employed there. A couple of them were in a state of undress and I remember thinking they looked like victims of famine with beautifully made-up faces and elegant coiffures and not a pick on their bones. Monsieur Balmain said something about needing bean-poles, not women. I was slim and shapely at the same time—not what he was looking for.

Although I was beautifully turned out that day, inside I felt like I didn't belong. I thought they were doing me a favor, just to meet with me, because I knew some of the Hollywood crowd. Even if I'd gotten the job, I probably would have done something to sabotage it. I was a genius at self-sabotage.

Sylvia included me in their lives and social activities. I met the writer James Baldwin several times, and we went on outings to restaurants together. Sylvia and I were secretaries of a committee Baldwin headed to collect signatures in support of Dr. Martin Luther King, Jr.'s planned March on Washington. A couple of weeks prior to Dr. King's march in August 1963, James Baldwin led a silent march to the American Embassy in Paris and presented the list of signatories who supported Dr. King's march. The symbolic Paris Civil Rights March was joined by many other expatriate artists, writers and actors. I met Richard Avedon, Memphis Slim, Hazel Scott and Anthony Quinn at some of the organizational meetings in the American Church on the Quai d'Orsay. Baldwin would later fly to Washington to join Dr. King.

I tried to break off the affair that I'd started with William in Dublin (and continued in Paris) when I found out that he and Sylvia were partners and lovers—but he wouldn't agree to it. I even wrote him a letter explaining my unhappiness with the situation, for I loved Sylvia dearly and did not want to hurt her. I never knew, and do not know to this day, whether or not she was aware of our affair.

Sylvia had been married to Paul Jarrico and had been an editor for the *Hollywood Quarterly*, which was published by the University of California. When the regents required all members of the staff to sign a non-Communist oath, Sylvia resigned. She would have been fired anyway for her refusal to sign. She and Paul were most famous for their work on the film *Salt of the Earth*, written by Sylvia's brother-in-law, Mike Wilson. Mike was a highly successful screenwriter who had been blacklisted, and was married to Sylvia's sister Zelma, who was a sculptor. I often went to the Wilsons' fabulous home in Pontoise, just outside Paris. One of my sidelines was working as a model for Zelma and some of her artist friends. I needed those sidelines, because I only worked at La Nouvelle Eve until it was time for the troupe to go to Buenos Aires for six months. Right before they left, I quit without telling anyone in the company I was leaving. I just disappeared.

Soon afterwards I was posing *au naturel* for Zelma and she noticed some marks on my body. "How did you get those dark marks?" she asked. I told her the truth. They were from love-making. She wanted to know who I'd been with, and I told her everything about me and William. I expected all hell to break loose, but instead my relationship with William ended very quietly. He simply told me they were moving to 94 Rue du Bac and that the new apartment would be too small for all three of us. Nothing else was mentioned. I was moved into a cheap hotel, courtesy of my benefactors, and the rent was paid up for two months in advance. When that ran out, I went home to Dublin. It was Christmastime and I was homesick.

A dozen or so years later, after I moved to San Francisco, I reconnected with William and Sylvia, who were living in the San Fernando Valley in California. They accepted me lovingly back into their lives and the three of us remained loyal friends and comrades until their deaths. When I wanted to apologize to Sylvia, William pleaded with me not to do it. Years later, I realized that was good advice. The apology would only have hurt her.

In 1987, twenty-four years after I'd written it. William returned to me the letter I had sent him in Paris when I was eighteen and trying to break off our relationship. He included a note saying that he'd kept it to better place his walks and thoughts from that period. I was surprised, because I'd forgotten all about the letter.

Dear William,

You know I find it hard to discuss things with you to your face and that I find it easier to put things on paper. I've already discussed a lot of my problems with Sylvia but I can't tell her that the biggest problem is you. I've hinted at it but the question of your being unfaithful is the farthest thing from her mind—so how can she suspect? Up to last night I thought she might be aware of my feelings for you, but obviously she is not.

The situation here is getting me down. It's never going to change unless I get a job on a full-time basis and contribute to Sylvia some of the money I feel I am costing her. I need to find some other friends who will take me out so the only time I will be in the apartment is to sleep. I love you very much and I think you have the same feelings for me. But the love you show Sylvia is the kind of love I expect based on how I feel about you. From time to time you show me what our life together could be and this hurts me more than if we just stopped kidding around. It will hurt at first but it will be better in the long run.

You've probably suspected I'm not entirely happy here, the reason being that I don't seem to be making any progress. I feel depressed because I can't do the kind of work I want to do. Working at La Nouvelle Eve or posing for Zelma is not what I want to do. I know to survive I have to do these things but I don't seem to be very successful. There seems to be no way I can get on my feet. If I could do the things I want to do I know I'd be happy and I know it would make you happy. I'm aware you have worries yourself about work but who else but you can I turn to for help. Cheer up you'll soon be away from it all.

Renée

William was getting ready to go to Africa to work in a film when I wrote that letter.

The last time I saw him, many years later, he was suffering with Alzheimer's disease. There were fleeting moments when he recognized me, but other times he'd ask, "What was I doing in Dublin?" It was quite sad, and the first time I'd experienced Alzheimer's close up. One morning as I was about to board a plane from San Francisco to Dublin, my daughter Aisling phoned me to say that William had died. He was seventy-eight. During one of my visits with Sylvia after William died, she told me some stories of his philandering. When I asked her why she'd put up with it, she said, "For the greater good." She was an extraordinary woman in every way, and never treated me with anything but love and respect. I'll never know what she did or did not know about my relationship with William.

Over the years, Sylvia and William collaborated on many projects and worked together to change the image of blacks in theatre and film. Thanks to them, blacks were more likely to be hired as actors and screenwriters, and not just as janitors. They took the one man show they developed, "Enter Frederick Douglass," to colleges, community centers and campuses around the country. It was also shown on PBS. William's lifelong dream, sadly unfulfilled, was to make a movie about Toussaint l'Ouverture the revolutionary leader of Haiti, which in 1804 became the first black-led Republic in the world.

Ironically, William became best known for the Blaxploitation film *Blacula*, and as the "King of Cartoons" on the 1980s television show, *PeeWee's Playhouse*. He continued to play Othello over the years, and in 1991 made a video of the play with Jenny Agutter as Desdemona.

In 2011, I went back to Paris and dropped in at La Nouvelle Eve. "Oh, were you one of The Mayfair Girls?" the manager asked, and invited me to take a look around. He rummaged through the archives, hoping to find a photograph of me back in the day. He asked me why I hadn't kept any of my publicity photos and I told him frankly, "I was an Irish Catholic, seventeen years old, who didn't want her family or friends to know what she was up to in Paris." I regret not having some record of all the fabulous costumes of feathers and glitter that I wore during my short stint there.

Walking through Pigalle where William had kept an apartment, I remembered how he would meet me outside La Nouvelle Eve after the show. We'd walk on down to Les Halles, the all night market, and have onion soup at four o'clock in the morning. He knew all the whores on the street corners and introduced me to them as his "little sister."

Hard to Bear

≈

When I was eighteen, just back in Dublin after my year in Paris, I joined the Betty Whelan Modeling Agency. I ran around with students from Trinity College and actors from the theatre and film communities.

By then I had reconnected with the young man who'd taken the photographs that helped me land the Paris job. He was working as a photojournalist with the daily newspaper. I slept with him after a game of strip-poker because I wanted to show off my beautiful Parisian lingerie. When I discovered I was pregnant, I went to his flat to tell him and found him in bed with my best friend. From there I went directly to his mother's house and told her about my plight. "You should have had more sense," she said and showed me out.

I didn't know where to turn. I knew my father would kill me if he found out. My mother would want to raise the baby. I didn't want my child to have a repeat performance of my own upbringing. I knew the boy would probably have married me out of duty, but I didn't want that life—my parents' life.

I took a modeling assignment traveling around Europe, doing trunk shows with a fashion designer from London—until my bump began to show. Dairin Quin from the Betty Whelan agency came to Paris to replace me, and I tagged along on the rest of the trip with her and the designer. I didn't know what else to do. The three of us traveled all over Europe and then hung out in London for a bit after the gig was finished. I had very little money and slept a couple of nights in Victoria train station with newspapers for covers.

After a few days of homelessness, I took the boat and train back to Dublin. I stayed a few weeks, just long enough to get a ticket back to Paris. When I arrived, I rented a cheap room in a student hotel on the Boulevard St. Michel. I knew William and Sylvia would have helped me—but when I went to their apartment, the concierge told me they'd returned to California. I turned to my Australian friend, Alison Farrell, who was working as an *au pair,* and she introduced me into her circle of Australian friends. One of them, a pilot named Mike Parer, took pity on me and gave me some money to relocate to England, where I could find work. He didn't know me from a hole in the ground, but he was a very compassionate man.

I went to England and tried to settle into a bedsitter in Notting Hill Gate in London. Besides the boy who fathered my child and his mother, I had told no one in Ireland I was pregnant. I spent the loneliest few months of my life waiting to give birth. Several times on the streets of London, I saw young girls I recognized from home who were also pregnant. But our shame was too great for us to acknowledge each other.

I worked at a theatre box office in the West End and went to a lot of movies alone. For months, I didn't have a real conversation. My sadness put people off. I never saw a doctor. I knew I was pregnant and that was all I needed to know.

I had already made up my mind to give the baby up for adoption and was in contact with an organization in Manchester that would make all the arrangements. How I got to Manchester is fuzzy in my mind. I just remember a boarding house with a kind older woman and her wonderful roast lamb and cauliflower dinners.

When I went into labor, I had no idea what was going on. I screamed, "I'm going to die." One of the lodgers in the boarding-house was a taxi driver and he took me to the hospital. I don't remember how long my labor lasted. When my son was born, I was not allowed to hold him or nurse him. The women in charge told me, "You don't want to get attached." At night, I could hear my little boy crying in the nursery but I was not allowed to pick him up. "You don't want to get attached," the women kept repeating. It was like that for ten days before he was adopted and I was discharged to go on my lonely way.

I'd sent Mammy a plane ticket to meet me in London and she arrived with my little brother Patrick in tow. He was only three at the time and couldn't be left at home. I thought I was looking very mumsy with my engorged milk breasts and a few extra pounds, and felt sure she would guess what I'd been up to.

I'd been hoping against hope that she would say something, so we could talk. But no! She said nothing. I was so sad and lonely. It wasn't until I started therapy in California that I dealt with the anger I felt towards Mammy for not recognizing I'd been pregnant. Regardless of the seven children she'd given birth to and nursed, she couldn't or wouldn't acknowledge what I'd been through. Was that deep denial? At the time, it didn't even occur to me that *I* could have said something to *her*.

Both behaving as if everything was normal we went to the Theatre Royal, Drury Lane, to see Laurence Harvey in *Camelot*. Then we went straight back to Dublin and I got a job with a travel agency. It lasted for a couple of years. I lived in a bedsitter on Northumberland Road, one street away from where I was born.

I gave my baby up for adoption partly because I knew the family history and I'd seen how scarred Mammy and Daddy were from being tossed around. I didn't want that for my child.

I got pregnant because I knew nothing about sex. Sex education was unheard of in our home or in the schools I attended. When I began menstruating I cried to my mother that I was dying. She said, "Don't worry, it's something you have to get. Otherwise you'll go crazy like that crazy Mary at the end of the street." Then she added, "Don't tell your father." That was the sum total of my sex education. She gave me a torn rag for a sanitary towel.

Every September 13th when my son's birth date comes around, I think of him and wonder if he is alive. Did he fight and die in the Falklands War or get blown up on the streets of Belfast or Derry? I've left a paper trail for him to find me, but I fear he may not know he is adopted.

Painful Losses

I am practically a teetotaler but every now and again I indulge myself. The first time I tasted good French champagne, it was like a religious experience. It was at my friend Mary's wedding in Dublin. I remember how happy we all felt dancing, singing, drinking champagne and crying at Mary's wedding. She was the first of a bunch of us girls who worked together to get married.

Mary was a delicate girl. When told that she shouldn't get pregnant because of her poor health, she and her husband asked the doctor for some form of birth control, but that was illegal in Ireland at the time and the doctor refused their request. The first time Mary had sex was on her honeymoon in Spain. She got pregnant right away and immediately the problems started.

She was ordered into Holles Street Maternity Hospital for the duration of the pregnancy. I remember vividly going to Sandymount Strand with the girls from work and digging cockles because Mary had a terrific craving for them. We brought them into the hospital in a large bucket, sprinkled them with salt and vinegar. Mary and the other women in the public ward feasted on the fresh cockles.

Mary had been hemorrhaging when she was admitted to the hospital, but the doctors would not abort the baby. They told her husband that if she had a second hemorrhage, she might die. It was well-known at the time, if ever a choice had to me made between the mother's life and the baby's life, the doctors at Holles Street Hospital would save the baby. They were just doing what every other Catholic hospital in Ireland was doing. Many children, too many to count, were left motherless because of this practice.

Mary had a second hemorrhage and then a third one. She and her unborn baby died, and she was buried the same year she got married. She was twenty-one years old.

Not long afterwards, one of Mary's friends went on a date with a very gracious older man to whom she had been introduced by a close friend. After a lovely luncheon together at a fine restaurant and one too many glasses of champagne, the worldly gentleman invited her to his place for a cup of tea. She was not interested in romance or sex with him, but he wanted to kiss and cuddle with her. When she refused, he got very angry and tried to pin her down and rip her clothes off. Her cries of help went unheard. Eventually, she broke loose and ran screaming from his flat.

She went to the nearest friend she could find in the neighborhood, a young man her own age who, under the pretense of consoling her, forced sex on her. The young girl was horrified when she found out she was pregnant. Abortion was illegal and after agonizing about what to do, she did like so many before and since have done. She boarded the mail boat for England and the abortion parlors of London. On the lonely way home from the abortion clinic, she stopped at a toy shop and bought herself a rag doll. She cried for the next twenty years.

I was that girl.

Seven Years Wandering

Although I couldn't wait to get out of Ireland, I was always homesick when I was away.

After giving up my son and having the abortion, I felt at sea. I couldn't seem to get a grip on my life, and felt I had no choice but to emigrate. I had to get away from the stranglehold of the Catholic Church, the economic poverty of the times and the loneliness of not fitting in.

(The Catholic Church had been in my bad books ever since my mother was threatened with excommunication. After giving birth to her sixth child she had decided that she would give up conjugal relations with her husband. At Confession, the priest gave her the old "marriage is for the procreation and education of children" bit and said nothing about how she was supposed to feed and clothe them. Contraception and abortion were still illegal in Ireland.)

Even though I knew I had to leave Ireland, I was of two minds about going. On the day I left, Mammy, whom I adored, and my brother Sean, whom I idolized, saw me off at Dublin Airport. I was flying to London and then on the Southampton, where I was to board a ship to Montreal. I remember thinking, "If there is a God, let him act now. Please, please, I beg you, make them ask me to stay." They hugged me good-bye. I turned away and couldn't look back. As I walked towards the plane, I felt my heart breaking in two.

I spent seven years moving restlessly among Ireland, France and Canada. I even took a stab at living in Rome, but it didn't pan out. I think of those years as my years of wandering in the wilderness. I couldn't settle in any one place and I did not know the reason for my unhappiness. I put up a good front. I had jobs where I got free or discounted travel, and that suited my lifestyle. I rented rooms in cheap hotels or stayed in boarding houses, and I was good at managing the little money I earned. I never owned a car. I would buy Mammy a plane ticket from time to time, and she would join me wherever I was. We would visit, and see a few plays or go to the opera.

During those seven years, I married a man I did not love just because he pursued me so relentlessly. He even followed me to Europe to beg me to come back to Canada. I let him talk me in to returning with him because I believed no one else would want me. I spent two years on and off in that dysfunctional and abusive marriage which ended in divorce.

It was only later in therapy, that I came to terms with the sadness and disorientation I felt in those seven years. I hadn't acknowledged to myself the pain I'd suffered around giving up my son for adoption and my feelings about the abortion.

Fate Takes a Hand

❧

When I was fourteen, I had nothing but contempt for marriage. I remember one day in school when we were learning about the "Holy Sacrament of Matrimony," I said to the priest who was teaching us, "I'm never getting married. I'll probably just live in sin with some older American man." The words just tumbled out of my mouth. I have no idea where they came from, but everyone was shocked.

As a matter of fact I'd never seen a happily married couple. At the time, I was angry that my mother was expecting her seventh child and still living in misery with my father. I used to say to my brother Sean, "Why in God's name didn't she leave him when she only had the two of us?"

Today I think that even if divorce had been legal, they would have opted to stay together. There is a kind of dance that couples do. Even though it can be deadly, they get so used to it that it becomes easier to continue than to quit. It is like the old adage, "Better the devil you know than the devil you don't know."

After my "seven years in the wilderness," I had pretty much made up my mind to live my life alone. I'd had too many bad experiences with men and relationships. When I was in my mid twenties, I felt a strong urge to have a child. When the opportunity presented itself, I did so with a man of my choosing with no commitment and no strings attached.

The birth of my daughter turned out to be the best thing that ever happened to me. Having to take care of another human being will wake you up in a hurry: there is nothing like it. I took a long inventory of my life and saw all the things I needed to change. I had to stop blaming my parents for everything and take responsibility for my own life. Shortly afterwards fate took a hand and threw me together with that "older American man" I had prophesied when I was fourteen.

I was living in Canada at the time, and my daughter Aisling was still an infant. I had a fascination with Alexandria, Egypt—the home of Cleopatra and the Alexandria Lighthouse (one of the Seven Wonders of the Ancient World) and the site of the greatest library the world had ever known. I'd read Lawrence Durrell's *The Alexandria Quartet* and, on a whim, decided to make a trip there. I was working in the travel business, so it wasn't such a far-fetched plan. My boss gave me the time off. I dropped my daughter in Dublin with my mother and spent a month travelling in Egypt.

I loved Alexandria so much that I decided to move there as soon as I could organize it. Two months later, I booked the trip at a quarter the minimum fare and then quit my job in Vancouver to go live in Egypt.

With my year-old daughter I boarded the P & O's *Oriana* for a three-week voyage along the west coast of America and through the Panama Canal to Europe. It was a beautiful spring day when we sailed under the Golden Gate Bridge and docked in San Francisco to pick up passengers and supplies. That was my first time in California. Somewhere near the Panama Canal, a couple from England introduced me to a fellow passenger named Lew, whom they thought I might like. He was a long-haired San Francisco radical, and we sat on the deck in the moonlight drinking champagne and Guinness and talking. A steward named Maurice from Cork took care of Aisling that evening, and many others.

When Lew first heard my name he said it sounded very familiar and we racked our brains trying to figure out how he could possibly know me. I had never been to San Francisco before. Finally the penny dropped. Two years earlier I had been on one of my relocations by ship and had lost my steamer trunk with everything I owned in the world—my Nina Simone and Leonard Cohen records, a copy of Shakespeare's *Hamlet*, a pair of Waterford Crystal goblets, and my treasured over-the-knee purple suede boots. Somewhere along my route there had been a labor dispute on the docks and my trunk got left behind. It ended up in Lew's locker at Pier 35 in San Francisco, where he was the baggage master. He'd had it there for six weeks while he tried to locate the Renée Jackson on the label. He told me that every morning he came to work the first thing he looked for was a forwarding address for that trunk. Eventually the P & O traced it and it later caught up with me in Dublin via Fort Lauderdale and Le Havre. I asked Lew if he believed in fate. He said our experience with the lost baggage was merely a coincidence.

Our moonlight talks continued over several nights. We were different in many ways, but our basic beliefs were the same and we began to develop great respect and admiration for one another. I found out a lot about Lew and discovered that he did more than just talk about his beliefs; he lived them. Lew had gone to Delano every weekend and marched in the grape boycotts with Cesar Chavez. In San Francisco he was at the sit-ins at the Palace Hotel and the car dealerships on Van Ness Avenue, fighting to have those places integrated. He was a founding member of Men for Peace and put together the first anti-Vietnam War rally in San Francisco that was not organized by students.

He was very involved in the trade union movement and also a great lover of the arts. A child of the Great Depression from a small town in New Mexico, he knew what it was like to be poor. His childhood experiences were not that different from those of a girl from the slums of Dublin. He lived through the Blacklist of the McCarthy era and was almost lynched once at the GM auto plant in Van Nuys, California, for his union activity there. We discovered he knew many of the people who had been my friends in the Paris days.

Lew told me he was interested in learning something about his ancestry. He had a few loose bits of information. His grandfather had left Ireland in the late 1800s and made his way to the mines of Montana. Once there, he had married a woman from the Blackfeet tribe and together they'd had thirteen children. He didn't have much more information than that. He wasn't searching for his roots, as they say; he was merely curious.

When we got to Dublin, he rented a Mini Minor and I offered to accompany him on his travels to show him the splendors of the place. Unfortunately for him, he had expectations of meeting a Kevin Barry or a Patrick Kavanagh in every town. In other words, he thought every Irish person would be a revolutionary or poet or both. We met nary a poet on any barstool between McDaid's in Dublin and The Plaid Shawl in Galway. There were oodles of raconteurs and fiddlers, but not an ounce of revolutionary thought amongst them.

"Where are all the revolutionaries?" he wanted to know, and I could not answer him.

In spite of that, he was having a great time. Since we couldn't find many people with whom to have fiery political discourse, Lew settled for solitary fly-fishing instead. For days, he fished without a nibble. One day out by a wild lake, we were enjoying the scenery and the fresh air when an old woman came walking towards us across the fields. I knew she'd been watching us all day from afar.

"Would yiz like to have a soft-boiled egg and a bit of brown bread?" she asked.

We said we'd love to and she led us back across the fields to her thatched cottage. With a fire in the hearth and a kettle on the boil, it was like a scene out of one of J.M. Synge's plays. The woman made tea to go with her homemade brown soda bread and the fresh eggs. When we were getting ready to leave, she pulled my companion aside and asked if he would like to make a donation towards "the tea." I could feel myself turn bright crimson from embarrassment, but he said to me, "It's okay. Isn't she a poor old woman? She had to buy the food. Why shouldn't she be helped out for her kindness?"

After our fly-fishing adventures, we took a small boat out to an island off the south coast. There were no commercial establishments there, but we were told to enquire at a cottage near the top of the cliffs. "If she likes you, she'll rent you her caravan for the night," someone told us.

I hiked up in my high heel shoes and one of the heels broke off. We knocked on the cottage door and a woman answered. Her husband stood behind her. "Ah, you've nearly ruined your shoes," he said when he saw the shoe in my hand. He went and got a hammer and some nails and fixed it. His wife was more interested in whether or not my companion and I were married. We both gave different answers at the same time, and she pretended to be deaf. She launched into a moral tale, but she rented us the caravan in any event. It was a magical setting on a lake with craggy cliffs a stone's throw away. The rocks were home to thousands of gannets and puffins. We walked the island and did some bird watching.

At Grogan's Pub in Dublin a few days later, news had already reached the city that I was traveling with a man and we were posing as a married couple. My friend thought that charming, whilst I tried to figure out what spy organization was tailing me.

I got to know my traveling partner very well during our six weeks together on the ship and in Ireland. He invited me to spend some time with him in San Francisco, and I did. I never did start a life in Alexandria .

On our subsequent visits back to Ireland, I wore a wedding ring and we were able to share a room, unlike that first trip when a woman at a B&B in Dublin told us, "I don't allow men to have female visitors. My husband patrols the premises at night, so don't try and pull any funny stuff."

Ah, Ireland, we love her and we hate her but she never leaves us.

Part 4
Elsewhere

❧

There's no pill or drug on the market that can cure me of the travel bug I've had since I was knee high to a grasshopper. Friends often ask me about what they call my obsession with travel. I'll let Robert Louis Stevenson speak for me: "For my part I travel not to go anywhere, but to go. I travel for travel's sake. The great affair is to move, to feel the needs and hitches of our life more nearly, to come down off the feather-bed of civilization and find the globe granite underfoot and strewn with cutting flints."

Poetry and Mystery

≈

I loved poetry as a girl. The romance of poetry and some of those exotic places mentioned in poems have inspired many of my travels. Mother Consolata, my teacher, must have had a romantic streak. As I look back on the poems she chose for us, I see there was a great longing in them. When I was ten years old, she seemed like an old lady—but when I reflect back on it now, I realize she must have been about twenty-eight.

Since childhood, I've always had one or two lines of particular poems going round and round in my head. One was:

Quinquereme of Nineveh from distant Ophir
Rowing home to haven in sunny Palestine.

To me, those are some of the most beautiful words I've ever heard, and it may be those very lines that gave me my love of words and my burning desire to see the world. I absolutely knew the person rowing home to Palestine was carrying precious cargo that included emeralds, white wine and peacocks.

Between contractions when I was laboring to give birth to my daughter, I began to recite from some primal place:

Aisling gaobhar do amharcas fein
Im leabaigh is me go lag briocht
Ainnir thaobh darbh ainm Eire
Ag teacht im dhaor ag marcaiocht
A suil rabhar glas
A cul trom cas....

Those were the only words that came to me. The remainder of the poem was a mystery. Loosely translated, it says that in a dream a beautiful maiden named Eire came riding towards me. She had round green eyes and a trim waist and a swan's neck, or words to that effect. It is from a genre called "*aisling*," or visionary poetry, from the repressive bad old times when the Irish were forbidden under pain of death to write about their country. There was usually some hidden political message within the poem.

Needless to say, the baby whom I had planned to name Vanessa, after Vanessa Bell, Virginia Wolfe's sister, became Aisling instead. She spells it phonetically now, Ashling, so people won't be confused by the Gaelic. I love it that the one word, Aisling, holds so much of what I love in life—my wonderful daughter and the poetry that inspires me toward the mysterious elsewhere.

Mrs. Purcell Saves the Day

꒰ꑂ

My first trip outside of Ireland was to Wales. I was almost twelve years old, a soloist in our school choir, and we had been chosen to sing at the Eistedfodd Music Festival in Llangollen.

My mother had made monthly payments towards the cost of the trip and it was all paid up—but when the big day came, I was unable to scrounge up enough money to pay my bus fare to the docks to catch the boat. No one on our avenue had a car. In those days, only the rich had cars. I can remember the knot in my stomach as the minutes ticked away and it looked like the trip would be lost to me forever.

I stood in front of our house with my little suitcase, hoping against hope that some miracle would happen, when our neighbor Mrs. Purcell walked down the avenue and waved to me. "Here, Renée," she said, "I wanted to give you pocket money for sweets or something." With that, she thrust a ten-shilling note into my hand. I charged up the road and hopped on the first bus I saw. I was the last person to board the Dun Laoghaire to Holyhead ferry. The sea was rough and everyone was sick.

The festival-goers were billeted in tents on a huge field with little cots to sleep on. All through the first night, we had torrential rains and woke up to find our belongings floating away in the flood. None of that dampened my spirits, though, and I did get to sing. I didn't know it at the time, but Paul Robeson, a person I admire greatly, also sang at that festival.

I used some of my ten shillings to buy cherries. It was the first time I had ever tasted cherries. Mrs.

MacGabhann, the choir director's wife, took a group of us on an outing: we floated down a canal on a barge, with a horse on either bank, pulling the barge along. The sun finally broke through, and I lounged there in the sunshine, in the middle of my first big adventure, eating ripe red cherries from a brown paper bag.

I was so happy, and couldn't wait for the day I'd leave home and see more of the world.

What Would Dervla Do?

❧

Fantasizing was one of my favorite pastimes when I was a child. Daydreaming was my escape from the travails of my home life. When I was ten years old, Geography was my favorite subject. I could draw freehand maps of many countries and dreamed of climbing their mountains and sailing their rivers one day.

At school, Mother Consolata used to run down the aisle between our little desks, swishing her bamboo cane and terrorizing all of her students. My major fault, according to her, was my habit of daydreaming. She'd call out my name and yell, "Come back from China at once, Renée Jackson." She wasn't far wrong in thinking I was dreaming about China.

Mother Consolata might be surprised to learn that I eventually made it to that faraway country. I took the Trans-Siberian Railway from Moscow to Beijing years before most people felt comfortable traveling in either the USSR or China. After a week on the train, I arrived in Beijing without a clue where I would find lodgings. I was armed only with a piece of paper that said in Chinese, "I need a room." I wandered out of the Beijing train station and went off to show my piece of paper to anyone who might be interested.

All one billion of the Chinese people seemed to be interested in me and my piece of paper. Everywhere I went, crowds gathered. A young boy seemed to be chosen to take me on a six-hour odyssey through the streets of Beijing on foot, by tram and by bus. He paid all the way and insisted on buying me ice cream. With not a word of any language in common, we eventually found a person with some authority (he was wearing a uniform) who gave me a voucher for a room.

Travel became my passion early in life. When I'm not traveling, I'm either dreaming about it or reading about other people's adventures. My favorite tales are by the brave and incorrigible Irish writer, Dervla Murphy. She does not let authority, weather, wolves or bandits impede her. In her books, she gives a list of the items she takes on her travels. Its bare bones stuff. Sometimes its true, she buys a donkey or a pony along the way, as she did when she took her six-year-old daughter trekking through the mountains of Pakistan in the winter months. But the animals are to pack things, like her daughter and her books of Shakespeare. She prefers to go on foot, lying down to sleep wherever she can, whenever she is tired, and eating whatever she is offered when she is hungry. She sometimes doesn't know what it is that she is eating or drinking. Often when I've gotten into tricky situations, I've asked myself, "What would Dervla do?"

When I was trekking in Nepal one time, I had Dervla's *The Enchanted Land* in my gear. It's about her stay in the Himalayas in the 1960s. I met a local man on a mountain pass and stopped to chat. His name was Buddhi. He spoke fluent English and said he was opening a library in his village. The next day, I walked for six hours through the high mountains in the thin air to donate the book to his library. I knew Dervla Murphy would be chuffed. A six-hour walk is nothing to her.

I've known some other intrepid travelers as well. My friend Barbara Navarro was my icon until I discovered Dervla Murphy's books. Barbara lives in Paris. She is an artist and activist involved in highlighting the plight of the Yanomami Indians to the outside world. The Yanomami are one of the largest isolated tribes in

South America. They live in the mountains and rainforests of northern Brazil and southern Venezuela.

Every winter, Barbara goes into the Amazon jungles for a couple of months. On her first trip, she flew to a small airport in Venezuela and hung around until someone asked her if she wanted to go down the river. She paid a boatman $200 and spent five days in a dugout canoe to get to a tribal village. She lived with the Yanomami for a time, and when she got home she wrote me letters on the backs of Xerox-copied photographs from her trip. In one picture, she is sitting in the canoe holding a monkey the way one would hold a baby. The next time I talked to her, I enquired about the monkey photo.

"I didn't realize a monkey would let someone hold it like that," I said.

"Of course, it wouldn't," she replied. "It was dead. We'd just killed it with a blowgun and were getting ready to skin and cook it."

Apparently, she had run out of her stash of canned sardines.

Jimi Hendrix at the Back of Beyond

Two yaks were coming straight at me on a very narrow trail. I prayed I'd have room to move aside without plummeting into the raging river below. I was at the rooftop of the world, looking for the Jimi Hendrix Café. I'd been told it was only slightly out of my way.

The yaks squeezed by me with inches to spare. I took a deep breath, fastened up my jacket against the snowy wind blowing down the gorge and forged ahead. It wasn't long before I spotted a hut with the words *Jimi Hendrix* over the door. I saw no people or activity of any kind—just the hand-painted sign on a door overlooking some of the most spectacular scenery on the planet. I snapped a photo, crossed a rickety suspension bridge over the Kaligandaki River and turned back to resume my original trek. It was just something I had to see, this throwback to the 1960s.

I'd finally made it to Nepal, a country that had been calling me for a long time. Is there a city anywhere more exotic-sounding than Kathmandu? I'd come to trek the Annapurna trail, never fully believing I'd be capable of handling it. I'd never been a jock or belonged to a gym. My exercise up to then had been walking the flatlands of Ireland and the hills of San Francisco. I'd worried that I'd not be able to walk up to twelve miles a day for eight days, as our group planned to do.

The trails were merely paths beaten down from animals and people traversing them for centuries. There are no roads for wheeled vehicles. Everything is hauled up either on people's backs or by yak, pony or mule. I saw men and women carry cages with hundreds of day-old chicks in them, whole trees for lumber, steel cables and all kinds of food. A young man carried an older man roped into a chair and tied onto his back. A woman walked alongside, holding an open umbrella over the old man to keep the sun's glare off him. Another day, a group carrying a corpse wrapped in a shroud and tied to two bamboo poles passed us on the trail.

A typical day would see our group of six up at 6:30 a.m. We'd walk from six to ten hours a day, depending on the terrain. At night we'd get a bed at an inn. It was $1 per person for a rough wooden cot with a thin foam rubber pad on top. You brought your own sleeping bag. Two people could get a room with a toilet and shower for $3. There was no hot water or heat. If there was any electricity at all, it wasn't powerful enough to read by. But most nights I was too tired to read anyway, after walking all day. We'd arrive at an inn, have a hearty meal for around $1 and get into our sleeping bags with all our clothes on. It could be very cold at night, even though days might be in the 70s.

Most of the people we met on the trail were Tibetans living in exile in Nepal. They were very friendly and curious about us. Their animals wore bells and decorative hand-woven saddles and intricate hair ornaments. It was a lovely sight and sound experience to encounter a caravan of animals on the trail, if a little daunting when you met them on a suspension bridge. Through all of it, we were surrounded by spectacular scenery.

The toughest part was a six-mile uphill climb that took me almost six hours in the rarefied air. It was the highest we would climb, about 14,000 feet. The town of Muktinath is a holy site for both Buddhists and Hindus and has magnificent snow-capped peaks on all sides. One of our group members had brought the ashes of a dear friend to cast into the sacred pools of the temple there, because the waters eventually find their way to the River Ganges in India. We had a brief ceremony and walked back to our inn at sunset with the sky coloring the snow pink and eagles flying home above us. At the inn, we ate at a communal table. The owner put some coals into a metal container under the table to warm us, for it was starting to snow outside.

From the jungle and savannah in the south up to the cooler climes, we saw alder, willow and apple trees, and wild watercress growing along glittering streams of melting ice as we climbed higher, with purple and yellow wildflowers scattered here and there along the paths. On the way back down from the heights, we saw marigolds, poinsettias and wild cannabis growing along the gorge. Surely there is no place on earth where Mother Nature puts on a greater show.

My body surprised me with its strength and resilience. I learned I'm healthier and more capable than I'd thought. I had no aches or pains or injuries and I thanked my body for that. But then amidst such charms of nature, who could harp on matters of fatigue, weariness or limitations.

A Critical Decision

❧

The Lost Coast of Northern California is part of the King Range National Conservation Area. It stretches thirty-five miles along the coast and includes 60,000 acres of old-growth forests, black sand beaches and a 4,000-foot-high wall of windswept peaks.

When Lew suggested we do a three or four day hike there, I knew it was extremely important to him. It was the last on a long list of "must-do" hikes that he wanted to complete while he still felt fit and able. The plan was to start near the town of Petrolia and hike twenty-five miles south along the beach to Shelter Cove.

In preparation for the trip, we'd ordered maps, tide charts and information on where we could pitch our tent each night. We had to plan by the tides and the moon. We would carry our tent, cooking utensils, food, water and the mandatory bear canisters in which to store our food. All in all, about twenty-five pounds for me, thirty pounds for him. We intended to walk seven miles the first day and camp by a creek.

We hadn't anticipated the difficulty of hiking on sand. It had not occurred to me beforehand to practice carrying twenty-five pounds on my back. I'm used to hiking with a day pack only. The going was tough as our feet sank into the sand. With a late start and the slow going, we feared we might not make it to our day's destination before dark.

We climbed up the cliffs and found a narrow trail above the beach that gave us better traction. It looked out at the wild ocean waves, and we saw elephant seals with their harems on the treacherous rocks way below us. As we maneuvered along the narrow ledge, I realized my gear was not evenly distributed on my back and I was veering to one side. I knew if I lost my balance, I'd be a goner. I was struggling, but at the same time determined to continue.

After walking awhile on that trail, Lew's knee gave out. He had injured it on a trek in New Zealand earlier that year. It just locked up on him and he couldn't bend his leg.

"I can't go on," he said. "It's too dangerous." He was disappointed, but he knew we had to turn back. We checked our map and found we'd only gone three miles on a hike that felt like ten, and it had taken about four times as long as we'd anticipated. Together we hobbled back to the trailhead. It was excruciating. Each time we rounded a curve and thought we were back to where we'd started there'd be another endless stretch of beach to navigate. We were so exhausted we couldn't even set up our tent.

We reached our car and drove until we saw some sign of life. We knocked on the farmhouse door, and asked for a bed for the night. The woman told us where we could get lodgings. The next day, we felt revived and were grateful we'd made the right decision to quit.

An artist I knew in Eureka drove out to some wild place to paint without telling anyone where she was going. She parked her car and walked a long way till she found a scenic spot that suited her. She soon realized she had left her water bottle back in the car and trekked back to get it. Arriving at the car she found, to her horror, that she'd left her keys out at the scenic spot with her art supplies. Somewhere in her going back and forth, she broke her foot. It was ten days before another hiker came down the trail and found her body and the note she had managed to scribble, explaining what had happened to her.

A Dream of Timbuktu

જ્

As I stood on the banks of the River Niger waiting for a boat to take me to Timbuktu, the extraordinary sight of a caravan of nomads on camels caught me off guard. All of a sudden, I was fighting back tears. There I was, on the threshold of realizing a dream I'd had since childhood. I had always wanted one day to visit the far-off city of Timbuktu.

The city has long been associated with remoteness, isolation and inaccessibility—a place that is beyond the back of beyond. Some people are surprised to learn that such a place really exists. Timbuktu is in Mali, a landlocked country in West Africa. The city was founded at the beginning of the 12th century by Tuareg nomads, most likely to store grain. It later became a trading center for gold, salt and slaves on the trans-Saharan trade routes. It was also a great center of learning, and had a renowned library and one of the finest collections of manuscripts in the Muslim world.

The city long fascinated European explorers, each one dreaming of being the first to reach the fabled city of gold. Scotsman Gordon Laing took that honor when he reached Timbuktu in 1826, but he was killed by a Tuareg spear when he tried to depart. Two years later, René Caillie, the son of a poor Parisian baker, was the first European since the Middle Ages to see the city and live to tell the tale. He had studied the Koran and learned Arabic so that he could pass himself off as Muslim.

As for me, I was on my way to the Festival au Desert, the Festival in the Desert, forty kilometers from Timbuktu. My brother Patrick and his girlfriend had met me in Bamako, the capital of Mali. We found an excellent driver and a reliable jeep to take us on the long and difficult journey from Bamako to Timbuktu, but the payoff was as good as gold. The mud city of Timbuktu did not disappoint, but the sights once we got out into the desert were even more spectacular.

We stood speechless amid startlingly white shifting seas of sand as far as the eye could see. No vegetation, no shade, no footprints—only the crisscross patterns left by the large black sand beetles. From time to time I saw on the horizon tribes of "Blue Men," as the Tuareg are called, arriving on hundreds of camels and horses with their riders wearing the best of gear, some in indigo robes, others arrayed in gloriously bright colors, still others wearing all black. Tents of leather and canvas were pitched in the dunes and made cozy with rugs and pillows and heavy blankets. Although it can be 100 degrees during the day, the desert at night becomes bitterly cold. People keep warm by lighting bonfires in the sand dunes.

A stage and lighting had been hauled out across the sand for the annual gathering of the Tuareg, at which they catch up on the news, have some camel races and listen to some of the finest musicians in the world. There would also be a forum on AIDS awareness associated with the Festival.

Mali is renowned for its musicians, and these gatherings attract both Malian performers and musicians from other African countries. Salif Keita, Habib Koite, Baba Salah, Tartit and Tinariwen were among the performers from Mali. Some of Tinariwen's music is all screaming guitars, with moments of only vocals and a drum sounding very much like traditional Irish music. (The language of the Tuareg is Tamasheq. It sounds nothing like Gaelic, but there are some primal sounds that link the two.) Tinariwen was formed in the refugee camps of Libya where the Tuareg were driven after all their camels and goats were killed by the civil war and drought in Mali. In Libya they traded in their lutes for electric guitars, rightly believing they could reach a larger audience.

There was no program advertised in advance, so I was completely surprised and thrilled to run into some musicians from Ireland. The desert came alive with everyone bopping to Irish jigs and reels played by Nollaig Casey's fiddle and Mary Bergin's pennywhistle. The people went mad for it. Liam O'Maonlai of Hothouse Flowers and Irish piper Paddy Keenan were also there. In one of the most vivid memories, a group of Tuareg women dressed in black from head to toe, sit on the white sands of the Sahara and learn a song in Gaelic from O'Maonlai. These women mimicked with perfect diction and sang along. Words can't describe it.

What struck me most was how much I'd been missing the communal experience of music and the circle of affection that goes with it. In a country with thirty-one different languages, I felt at home. It was the all-time best tonic—experiencing the joys of community and dancing in the moonlight from dusk till dawn on the white sands with a million stars shining down.

I made a trip back to Timbuktu the following year to hear the incredible music and in the hopes of meeting up with some of the local folks I'd met the first time out—and I'd recruited some people to join me on my second journey. There was Roy, a guy from Belfast I'd found through the Internet, and Nadya, an old friend from North Beach. I met Sherry at Bimbo's nightclub on my birthday when I'd gone to hear Mariam and Amadou, a husband and wife musical team from Mali, and asked her if she'd be interested in going to the Sahara with me. She signed on right away.

My curiosity about Mali began several years ago when a close friend married a Malian named Sounkalo. His tiny village did not have a school, and he had been singled out as the one child to get an education at a school far from home. The villagers paid for his schooling collectively, with tomatoes, cucumbers, onions and whatever else they could grow and contribute. From these beginnings, Sounkalo eventually received a Ph.D. in robotics and now teaches at a university in France.

The second trip turned out to be a little tougher than the first one. In Mopti I had a mishap as I climbed onboard a *pinnasse* (the long motorized wooden canoes with curved-up ends that serve as transportation down the Niger River) I stepped with all my weight into a hole that had been covered over by a rattan mat. I fell flat on my back, twisted my spine and cracked my skull on an iron bar. I saw stars, got a terrible metallic taste in my mouth and passed out. There was no blood, though. When I felt the bump rising on the back of my head, I bawled my eyes out for about five minutes. Then I took a Motrin and tried to accept the fact that there was no ice available this side of the Tropic of Cancer. By the time we got to Timbuktu two days later, I had a raging migraine that knocked me flat. A doctor from Cuba, of all places, gave me some rehydration medicine.

I recovered, and completely enjoyed my second Festival au Desert. Tinariwen had just finished playing when I came across Salim and Joudu, some friends I'd made the year before. They were just folding their tents and readying their camels for the five-day ride back to their camp. I felt a bit embarrassed when I offered them the gifts of a couple of Timex watches I'd bought cheaply at Walgreens in its "after Christmas" sale. I said something dumb like, "I feel weird giving you a watch because perhaps you only travel by the stars."

Salim held the watch to his heart and said, "This is the most beautiful gift I have ever received."

It was amazing to be back in Timbuktu and have people recognize me in the street from the previous year. Some people even bought me mint tea and gave me gifts. The group of us went to the Sahara Passion to hear some live music. A Tuareg youth named Issaw, bedecked in indigo robes and veil, came and sat with me. He said he'd seen me at the Sahara Passion the year before and asked if I'd like to dance. I introduced him to my friends Sherry and Nadya and all of us danced together. Sherry and Issaw became friends and started a romance, and we invited Issaw to travel through the Dogon country with us.

(He and Sherry fell in love and nine months later their daughter Savanna was born. Issaw was an artisan who made jewelry and hand-tooled leather boxes. He worked from time to time restoring manuscripts in the library of Timbuktu. He hoped to come to America to work at a museum in Memphis and, sadly, died of malaria before the trip came to pass. Sherry and I were told about his death very casually some time later. "Oh Issaw died of malaria," our Malian friend said. Death is so commonplace there, and life expectancy so low, that someone dying is not considered a big deal. I was shocked and saddened that such a vital, healthy young man could be felled by malaria. I was also sad for Savanna, who would never meet her dad.)

After our visit to the Dogon country, we were supposed to go to Sounkalo's tiny village. I expected that to be one of the highlights of the journey. Sounkalo warned me that the village was difficult to get to and I got a sense of how remote and impoverished it was when I wrote asking what gifts I could bring his parents. He replied, "A bag of sugar, a bag of salt and a bag of soap would be really useful."

Unfortunately, the driver of our jeep didn't really want to make such a long trip and instead pretended he was having car trouble. He stranded us in Segou. We had to take a harrowing trip back to Bamako on a local bus—eleven hours on dirt roads, five of them in the dark, with sixty people and all their belongings, including goats and chickens and several large canisters of gasoline. A man beside me vomited on my shoes. I wasn't sure I would ever make it back to Bamako.

It was four o'clock in the morning when we arrived. I told myself "You are not sixteen anymore and perhaps it's time to travel with a few more creature comforts." I knew I'd get over the experience in time and remember only the beautiful parts.

I never made it to that village, but I enjoyed walking around the streets in Bamako and giving away the ton of soap I had carried all the way from Costco in San Francisco. Meant for my friend's parents, it was greatly appreciated by the women who make a living washing and dying clothes in tubs on the street corners of the capital.

High in the Himalayas

༄

I had wanted to go to Tibet since reading *Three Years in Tibet*, by Ekai Kawaguchi, a Japanese monk who traveled there in the late 1800s. He was one of the first outsiders to visit that secret country, which was isolated both by its government and by its mountains. Kawaguchi wanted so badly to get to Lhasa and read the Buddhist manuscripts in their original form that he spent a year in Darjeeling, India, studying Sanskrit, Chinese and Tibetan so he could pass himself off as a Chinese Buddhist monk. Tibet was a closed society for centuries. The only people who could pass through were a few of Chinese origin.

This brave, hearty, determined Japanese monk set off on foot for Lhasa with two sheep to carry his luggage all the way from Northern India through the Himalayas to Nepal and Tibet. He ate whatever food he could buy or beg along the way and asked for shelter from camping nomads to escape the cold, thin night air at high altitudes. One of the mountain passes he crossed was 22,650 feet above sea level, and of course he had no oxygen tanks. The complete adventure took six years; three of those were spent in Tibet.

My heart raced when I read his description of seeing 3,000 monks in one of the great rooms of the palace, arrayed in brightly-colored brocade robes and elaborate headdresses, chanting and meditating by the light of over a million yak-butter candles. I had to see Tibet.

I finally got there, and saw the thirteen-story, 1,000-room Potala Palace, the former home of His Holiness the Dalai Lama. I also visited the library of the Sera

Monastery, where Kawaguchi studied the scriptures. Standing outside the Palace, a tourist came up to me and asked, "Did I see you eating in a restaurant in Opatija, Croatia, last March?" We stood and talked about our respective travels—past, present and future— and exchanged addresses and telephone numbers as intrepid travelers do.

The Tibetan people are gentle and very beautiful with their elaborate dress and jewelry. They spend a lot of their time making pilgrimages, praying, worshipping and waiting for the return of their beloved exiled Dalai Lama. It has been against the law since "The Peaceful Chinese Takeover of Tibet" (as it is called) in 1965 to speak of the Dalai Lama or to be in possession of an image of him.

Lhasa is at 14,000 feet and the air is very thin. I'd been in the Himalayas before and had felt no ill effects in Kathmandu and even higher altitudes. This time, though, I was quite sick for the first day—perhaps because I was not as young as I had been, or maybe because I was already ailing with a respiratory infection from the extreme air pollution everywhere else in China.

A doctor was summoned to set me right. I had an excruciating headache, combined with incessant vomiting and nosebleed. I didn't want to die up there—but I told my husband that if I did die, just to leave me there and let the Tibetans do a "sky burial" of my body. They chop you into pieces and leave you out on the mountains for the vultures to feed on. It was only a fleeting idea, and I admit to being a drama queen. After the doctor came to the inn where I was staying, tied an I.V. to the bed post and gave me a shot, I was as right as rain in about a day and able to enjoy the rest of the trip.

The day I checked out of the inn in Lhasa, the lobby was full of tourists. Right there in front of everybody, a woman came out from behind the front desk holding up a condom and demanding that I pay for it because I had used it. (Condoms are left in your room for sale, if one feels inclined to use one.) I told her I'd had no use for a condom, that I felt so sick I'd barely known my own name and that I certainly had not been thinking about sex. She held it up like Exhibit A and showed it to everyone in the lobby. She pointed out how the corner of the wrapper had been torn back (I wonder who did that?) to prove the package had been opened. I forked over 100 yuan, a little over a dollar—a cheap price to pay for a good belly laugh and a yarn to spin at the end of the day.

Such a Shame

❧

When my daughter was young, my husband and I had an old van that we used as a camper. We had a mattress in the back where we'd sleep instead of using a tent. We had many a happy trip in that van and spent as much time as we possibly could in the countryside.

When we were first married and my husband suggested a camping trip, I went into the horrors. I'd grown up in a city and had always lived in big cities, so camping was not a part of my culture or my consciousness. I have this little fear mechanism that switches on when I'm about to embark on something I've never done before, when I'm stretching myself beyond my comfort zone. Then I often find, to my surprise, that the event is nowhere near as difficult as I'd anticipated.

I embarked on our initial camping trip to the Mendocino Coast moaning and complaining all the way. What a surprise I had in store! This was not a weekend of trail mix and powdered eggs. No! The first night, my husband cooked mussels in white wine, garlic and parsley for dinner. He had gathered the mussels from the rocks earlier that afternoon and I had watched with my heart in my mouth as the huge waves broke over him.

While we were doing that, our friend Mike Mullen had been out gathering mushrooms and had some beautiful chanterelles to contribute to the dinner. We cooked spaghetti on a primus stove and had a wonderful feast. I knew right away I could adapt to this lifestyle.

When my husband had first mentioned camping, I'd been thrown back to a time when, as a child of seven or eight, I was shipped off to a summer camp outside of

Dublin called Sunshine Home. It was for poor inner city kids and was run by nuns. We slept in dormitories patrolled by the nuns in their black habits and their jangling beads. I can still hear the creaking floorboards and see the dark shadows. I can still smell the huge white greasy sausages and the other horrible dreck they tried to feed us. We were given scratchy old woolen bathing suits that came to our knees, in the style of the 1920s, to wear to the freezing cold beach of Balbriggan.

I staged a hunger strike, even though I wasn't aware of the old Gael tradition that if you had a gripe against someone, you starved yourself to death on his doorstep. That was supposed to show him! Anyway, I staged my hunger strike and I suppose my parents were written to and told to come and get me.

My daughter Aisling was sent off to summer camp at about the same age as I was when I went to Sunshine Home. I thought her experience would be totally different from mine. First of all, I was able to pay for camp. It was not a charity deal and it was in the beautiful redwood forests of Mendocino County—the same area that we had come to love on our own camping trips. Only a few days had passed when we received a letter from her that started, "Dear Mom and Dad, I suppose you think I'm having a good time here. Well, I'm not!"

I couldn't imagine why she'd be so unhappy. After all, the camp was run by Wavy Gravy, that famous clown, hippie, philanthropist, philosopher, ice cream flavor, and all around good-guy. When the two-week camp was finished, her dad and I drove up to Mendocino to pick her up at Camp Winnarainbow. We didn't recognize the child they told us was ours. She had refused to wash herself or comb her hair for two straight weeks and was as black as a chimney sweep. She had dreadlocks in her waist-length blonde hair and I had to take a scissors and cut the knots out when we got home.

Since then, she has refused to talk much about her camp experience. Over the years, I've tried to pry some information from her—but all she will say is, "Nobody liked me. It was total anxiety." She said she enjoyed the horseback riding, however.

Next year, Aisling's daughter Alanna, will be the same age as we were when we first went to summer camp.

"Will you send Alanna to summer camp next year for her rite of passage?" I asked Aisling.

"Only if she begs me," she replied.

The Irish along the Mississippi

I've been in love with boats and trains, oceans and rivers ever since I rambled over to Wales from Dublin when I was twelve years old and floated down a canal on a barge. Rambling is just the right speed for me and I avoid jet planes as much as possible. I've floated down some of the great rivers of the world, including the Danube, the Nile, the Mekong, the Rhine, the Seine, Orinoco, Amazon and the Yangtze.

I spent a week on a paddle-wheeler going from New Orleans, Louisiana, to Vicksburg, Mississippi, and back again—a short distance that took eight days. I was on the *Delta Queen*, a steamboat built by an Irishman named Jim Burns in 1926. The *Delta Queen* originally operated between San Francisco and Sacramento, a trip that took twelve hours and cost fifty cents.

Our journey was quiet, and there is no better place for reflection than floating down a river. I like to sing as I float. On that trip, I was thinking of all the beautiful songs Ireland has produced and how the Irish have traveled to every part of the world. We have married with native populations and, when called to do so, have fought in the liberation of the countries we visited. I began singing a song that has haunted me since I first heard Kevin Brennan sing it in the Starry Plough in Berkeley. As I sang, I wondered again what sensitive lad had written such a beautiful song.

It was on a fine March morning, I bid New Orleans adieu
And I took the road to Jackson town, my fortune to renew.
I cursed all foreign money, no credit could I gain

Till I fell in love with a Creole girl
By the lakes of Pontchartrain.

When I got off the boat in New Orleans, I took the bus to Lake Pontchartrain. I was not on a quest of any kind—but as luck would have it, I found a grail of sorts. Standing in a field en route to the lake was a large Celtic cross. I learned that it marked a mass grave that had been unearthed in the late 1980s. It was dedicated to the Irishmen who died building the six-mile New Basin Canal that links Lake Pontchartrain to the Mississippi River.

Twenty to thirty thousand Irish came to the Louisiana frontier between 1830 and 1838. Those who survived the hardships of the journey were hired for fifty cents a day to do back-breaking labor in temperatures that often exceeded 100 degrees. There was no dynamite in those days; everything was done by hand. If you have ever seen the swamps in Louisiana, you have an idea of what torture that must have been. Besides the mosquitoes, snakes and alligators, the workers faced cholera, typhoid and yellow fever. They had no resistance to these diseases. Eight thousand men died and were buried where they fell along the ditches they were digging.

The Irish were actually known along the Mississippi much earlier than the 1800s. The Choctaw and Natchez tribes knew them well, and Gaelic may well have been the first foreign tongue that those indigenous people heard.

Paris, Mon Amour

In spring, one's thoughts often turn to love—and if not to love, then to Paris, the city of love.

Paris is no stranger to me, so even when I can't go there physically, I can conjure up the city in my mind with no trouble at all. The beautiful light at dusk, the walkways along the Seine and couples kissing under the arches, the best food and wine in the world, the museums filled with the finest treasures, the booksellers along the quays, the great flea markets, the Eiffel Tower with its twinkling lights, the lilac trees, Shakespeare & Co. bookstore and the Parisians with all their idiosyncrasies—these are the things that make Paris what it is.

I recently read a quote by George Whitman, who now owns Shakespeare & Co. The best possible circumstance, he said, is that of a young girl in love in Paris in the springtime. I immediately went to search for a photo of that eighteen-year-old girl who had been in love in Paris in the springtime, and took a good look at who I used to be.

My mature self had a new appreciation for the girl in the photo. I wondered why I'd had so little confidence back then, not only in my looks but in the spirit and gumption it took for an impoverished seventeen year old to venture out to a country where she'd never been, where she couldn't speak its language, and where she'd be dependent on the kindness of strangers. What I looked like and how I felt were completely at odds. People who knew me back then tell me I seemed very self-assured and sophisticated, but I was just going through the motions of having it all together.

Although my heart was broken in Paris, it was a small price to pay for all the growing up I did there. My mind was opened up to thinking and discussing and debating. I met artists and intellectuals I would never have known otherwise and Paris became something more than beauty and couture and gastronomy. I learned about politics and literature and anarchy.

So I'll go to Paris in my mind or in real time, and I'll walk past the Bastille where the rebels stormed the ramparts and started the revolution that promised "Liberté, Egalité, Fraternité" and inspired the people of Ireland to try a revolution of their own. I'll stroll on down the Seine and take a look in on the dinosaurs and the giant Irish elk at the Jardin des Plantes. I'll continue along past the Hotel Dieu, where Marie Antoinette was incarcerated. Then I'll go to Shakespeare & Co. to buy a couple of secondhand books and walk across one of the bridges to the Marais district and have escargots at Ma Bourgogne, my favorite corner restaurant on the Places Des Vosges.

Paris in the spring—Ooh La La.

Part 5
Characters

❧

One of the best things about longing for elsewhere—and then traveling elsewhere, even if it's only in your own neighborhood—is that you meet a host of fascinating characters. Their stories are inspiring, sad and funny. Each one of these extraordinary characters has enriched my life.

Joyce's Day

~

"If *Ulysses* is not worth reading, then life is not worth living." So said James Joyce about his masterpiece, which would transform all of 20th century literature.

Almost any conversation about *Ulysses* includes this admission, "I never managed to read it. Tried several times but somehow couldn't finish it." It's a pity that more readers don't persevere, because the book shouldn't just be the domain of scholars. The people about whom it was written were the ordinary people of Dublin. Joyce once said, "Nobody in any of my books is worth over a hundred pounds."

Ulysses took seven years of unbroken labor, 20,000 hours and more than 350,000 words to complete. It wreaked havoc on Joyce's eyes and nervous system. Unbelievably, he only had one-tenth of normal vision.

Each year, readers the world over celebrate what has become known as Bloomsday—June 16, 1904—the date Joyce chose for the fictional eighteen-hour odyssey through the labyrinthine streets of Dublin by the Irish Everyman Leopold Bloom. On that day Joyceans gather together and read aloud the words of their idol.

For some years, I have produced Bloomsday events at various venues around San Francisco. An even bigger, more elaborate Bloomsday celebration was scheduled for the centennial in 2004. For the better part of May and June, it felt like my life was being taken over by James Joyce. *Ulysses* in the kitchen, *Finnegan's Wake* in the bedroom, *Dubliners* in the dining room, and various poems and splayed-open books on, by, or about Joyce scattered, open, throughout the apartment.

Many people I know have "Joyce stories." I had a dear friend named Pele, a San Franciscan whose father owned a smuggled copy of *Ulysses* from when it was still banned. He was determined to meet the author one day. Pele's Aunt Muriel happened to play piano at the famous Boeuf sur le Toit in Paris and knew the restaurant where Joyce usually ate lunch. With only that scrap of information, Pele's dad booked passage by ship and rail from San Francisco to Paris. The year was 1926 and Pele was still a child. Off they went *en famille* to search for James Joyce in Paris, Pele's dad clutching his illegal copy. He found Joyce having lunch at a corner table, alone, as he often was, in Le Petit Trianon café. Pele remembered sitting to one side as her father chatted with "the man with the eye patch."

Years later, Pele's dad told her about his conversation with Joyce. Their discussion was not about literature, publication problems or libel, but about their mutual eye problems. Joyce gave Pele's dad the name of his ophthalmologist in Paris.

Turning a Blind Eye

In the glorious days of our courtship, Lew asked me, "How are you going to handle my drinking?"

I replied with more than a little bravado "It's no problem. I've had plenty of experience with drinkers." It was true, but I seemed to have forgotten just how that experience turned out. I suppose some warning bells should have gone off when I first met Lew. He was traveling with two suitcases, one with clothes and one with several bottles of tequila and fresh limes he'd picked up when the ship docked in Acapulco.

After our six-week romance—three weeks on the ship and three weeks touring around Ireland—we thought there might be something more to our relationship, so he invited me over to see if we still felt the same way about each other.

Everything went well during our visit and I moved to San Francisco to be with him. In all honesty, his drinking habits were not as bad as my father's had been, and my father's drinking was the yardstick by which I measured all drinkers. I was not a drinker myself, for what reason I don't know.

My love and I got married, but it wasn't exactly the wedding of my dreams. Lew and I had been cooking for the reception for three days. We'd gone fishing and had caught two salmon, twenty-six and twenty-eight pounds. We were smoking one and doing the second one in aspic. The night before the wedding, we had gone to hear Richie Havens and got home about two in the morning. We stayed up most of the night taking care of the salmon-in-aspic project because it had to be turned every fifteen minutes.

In the morning I didn't have time to wash my hair. When I looked in the mirror, I knew that was not the way I wanted to look on my wedding day. Lew and the best man, Mike Mullen, had been drinking gin fizzes since the crack of dawn. By the time they reached City Hall, they were not a pretty sight. Later, back at our apartment, Mike passed out in the middle of the dining room floor during the wedding celebration. I acted as if everything was normal.

Because my husband was not a violent drunk and because I didn't have to chase after him to get money for food, I let a lot of stuff slide. As anyone who lives with an alcoholic knows, the disease gets worse as time wears on. We went through the ugliness of the lies about how much he really drank and all the other problems that arise around alcoholism.

This went on for several years until an amazing thing happened. Mike Mullen, our best man, got sober. The general belief was that Mike was the worst drunk anyone had ever known. When we were invited to celebrate his one-year anniversary of sobriety at his home up in Eureka, I went but my husband found some excuse to stay home.

I'd never been to a party where there was no booze. We had music and laughter, great conversation and wonderful food. Over that weekend at Mike's house, I thought back to all the problems of a childhood in an alcoholic household—and I tried to think forward to what my life might become.

After my weekend away, I knew I had to give my husband an ultimatum. I only said it once: "You have to choose between me and the booze." He hasn't had a drink since that day.

Nothing is Simple

❧

When Aisling was nine years old, she came home from rehearsal with the San Francisco Girls' Chorus and said, "I've been invited to sing for the Queen of England! I'm sorry, Mom. I know how you feel about the Queen and the troubles in Northern Ireland."

I told her I didn't want her to do the concert. I think I may have said, "Your ancestors will be turning in their graves." There had been a thousand years of fighting between the island of Ireland and Britain. I was raised in a household with a motto, "Burn everything from England except the coal." That sentiment did not apply to ordinary Britons, only to the monarchy and the government.

After weeks of discussions Aisling announced, "Mom, I've made my decision." She went on "I've never sung for a queen before and I've never been in a place as beautiful as Davies Symphony Hall. I'll be singing with Tony Bennett and Mary Martin and may never get an opportunity like that again." I understood her reasoning, but I was frustrated with her at the same time. She stood her ground.

When the big day came, I told her, "I'm sorry I won't get to hear you sing." I meant it. The police were predicting that thousands of demonstrators outside Davies Symphony Hall would call for Britain to withdraw her troops from Northern Ireland. I would be with the demonstrators. I arranged for Aisling to spend that night with my friend Pat, because I knew it would be impossible for us to find each other in the crowds afterwards.

The next day, there was a special color edition of the *San Francisco Examiner* honoring the Queen's visit. Smack in the middle of the page was a photo of an angelic-looking child amongst a throng of demonstrators. It was my darling girl carrying a sign she had painted earlier that day and hidden in the bushes outside Davies Symphony Hall. The sign showed children skipping rope and bouncing a ball. There was a hammock strung between lush green trees, a bird smelling some flowers, a big yellow sun and a rainbow. Above them all she had written in crude black letters "NO WAR."

A Brave Soul

&

For about five years I was a volunteer at The Shanti Project, an organization that provides emotional and practical support to people living with life-threatening illnesses. That's where I met Jerry.

Jerry was a homeless speed addict who was diagnosed with HIV just as he had gotten himself off the streets and into a 12-step program. Time and again Jerry would be admitted to San Francisco General Hospital, so sick it seemed he would die. But each time he would miraculously improve and be discharged. Finally, they told him that the end was near and put him on a waiting list for a bed in a hospice.

His doctor told him, "Jerry, quit fighting so hard. It's time to surrender."

Jerry had been very open with me. We'd had many talks about death and the dying process. He had strong Christian beliefs and always said he was not afraid to die. On one of my visits, he was hardly able to speak. He couldn't eat or drink, and had been dry-heaving all day. I rubbed his back and stroked his hair as he tried desperately to vomit. He started to cry. "I'm scared. I'm so scared, Renée, I don't want to die alone." I didn't know what to do for him, so I lay down beside him and held him.

Crying myself, I wondered if it was the day he would finally surrender, or if he would keep holding on until his son and daughter found it in their hearts to come see the father they hadn't forgiven for being gay.

That turned out not to be Jerry's day to die. On a subsequent visit, out of the blue, he asked me. "Would you and your daughter sing at my memorial service?" He'd never even heard us sing.

"How about having your memorial service before you die?" I asked him. He thought that was a fabulous idea. We had the party two weeks later. By then Jerry was in a wheelchair and had lost the sight in one eye.

When he arrived, I led the guests in a chorus of his favorite song, "Fools Rush In." We settled into what turned out to be an incredibly inspiring evening. There was a reading from *Leaves of Grass* and several renditions of some old Irish airs. We sang "Eagles' Wings" and "His Eye is on the Sparrow" because Jerry loved birds. We continued with "The Rose" and "Somewhere over the Rainbow." His closest friends gave testimonials and told him how much they loved him. Jerry reflected on his life and kept us laughing with reports of some of its funnier moments. We ended the evening with "Amazing Grace" and everyone went home feeling joyful. That night Jerry got a new lease on life and surprised everyone, including himself, by living for another fourteen months.

Red-Headed Dave

When red-headed Dave rang my doorbell, I was surprised to see him alive. "Any mail from Chicago?" he asked.

"No," I told him. "But I've got lots of mail from the police, a summons to appear in court and several ambulance bills for you."

I've known Dave for about eight years. I met him in Washington Square not long after he first arrived in San Francisco. He was a good-looking young guy, thirty perhaps, with curly red hair and eyes of China blue. He was dressed in nice denim to match his eyes and was always plugged into a Walkman. He bopped around North Beach, smiling and waving at each person he met. Everyone liked him. He had a great sense of humor.

When we met, Dave told me he was trying to get back to Reno, where he had met a girl. He had lost a few teeth since he last saw her and asked me if I would help him get them fixed. I took him for free work at a dental school. He was like a little kid in more ways than one, and was terrified of the dentist.

"I'm not like the rest of those homeless guys," he told me. "I'm just interested in having a few cigarettes and some nice sounds for my Walkman." I would see him laundering his extra set of clothes at a place on Grant Avenue. He worked hard to maintain his Joe Cool demeanor even though he lived on the streets.

Dave asked me if he could use my address to get his social security check and I signed some forms for it. Once a year at Thanksgiving, he got a letter from his father with $50 cash to be spent on a turkey dinner and to be kept a secret from his mother.

It didn't take too long for Dave to lose his dignity and pride. Pretty soon after landing on the streets, he was getting drunk all the time. Sometimes he would show me the Greyhound bus ticket that would get him back to Reno and the girl who was waiting for him there.

One day he got picked up by an ambulance, and the doctor told him his liver was shot and he wouldn't last six months. Dave fell into a deep depression. It was Christmastime and he kept saying he wanted to be with his family. On his behalf I phoned his mother in Chicago to ask if he could come home. She called back a few days later saying no. But the people at Sts. Peter and Paul's Church helped work something out. He got on a plane to Chicago, having promised not to drink or use drugs while he was there. No sooner had he arrived than his mother put him on a bus back to San Francisco.

"I only smoked a joint and my mother got on my case. I told her she should have a smoke herself and lighten up," he told me. Still, he was happy that he had gone home for Christmas. But the annual Thanksgiving letter never came again.

As Dave's health problems got more serious I communicated with his parents on and off. But finally they moved and left no forwarding address, or telephone number. His sister remarried and Dave didn't know her new name.

Dave took up with a homeless woman named Judy and moved from Washington Square down to her stomping grounds at Civic Center. Occasionally I'd run into them at Union Square. I'd get ambulance bills and warrants in both their names. They'd been beaten, run over by cars and fallen out of buildings. You name it, it happened to one or the other of them. A few months later, Dave came by to say he had awakened to find Judy dead beside him.

I don't know how or why Dave is still alive. He's back in my neighborhood now after a seven-week stint in hospital.

"Any mail from Chicago?" he calls up the stairs. I tell him no.

Thanksgiving in the Park

My Thanksgiving observance started several years ago when Timmy, one of the homeless people who live in my neighborhood, asked me if I would save him the leg of the turkey. I didn't have the heart to tell him that I don't celebrate Thanksgiving. Every morning of every day leading up to Thanksgiving, Timmy would give me that count-down, grinning like a Cheshire cat. "Only three more days to Thanksgiving!" "Only two more days to Thanksgiving!" So I told him I would cook a turkey for him and the rest of the guys and deliver it to Washington Square at 7:30 on Thanksgiving morning.

Most of the guys in the park are alcoholics and drug addicts, and many of them are Vietnam vets. I have gotten to know them and some of their stories over the years. They live on the edge and are out there trying to survive as best they can. Most of them are unable to hold down a job or function in a relationship because of their addictions, but for the most part they are very sensitive souls. These homeless men and women who live in our city, some mother bore them.

Thanksgiving came around and my husband and I stayed up most of the night cooking a huge turkey. We went all out, making stuffing, mashed potatoes, gravy, fresh cranberry sauce, bread and butter and filling up flasks of coffee. We brought the dinner down to the park at the crack of dawn, because any later and those guys would be too loaded to care about food. Timmy was passed out when we arrived. Maybe he hadn't really believed the dinner was going to materialize. Maximilian, who was the "grand old man" of the group, promised to save the leg for Timmy.

So we left the food with them to enjoy in whatever way they wanted and went home to catch up on our sleep. It was a great hit and became a yearly tradition.

I used to see Timmy every morning when I went to Washington Square to do Tai Chi. I dialed 911 for him many times and saved him from choking on his tongue when he was having an alcoholic seizure. One time, I took him to San Francisco General when he needed surgery. He struggled something terrible with his alcoholism but somehow managed to get sober several times over the years I knew him. During one of his sober times, he got a room in a hotel for a while and some relatives got him a job at Fisherman's Wharf. He cleaned up and had a loving girlfriend, but it didn't last. He just couldn't stay away from the drink.

The last time I spoke with Timmy, I was on my way to a wedding party in Berkeley and he reminded me to save him some of the leftovers.

I left to visit Ireland right after that. When I got back, I went down to Washington Square to catch up on the latest news. Red-headed Dave was sitting on the bench by the bus stop, plugged into his Walkman as usual.

"How's it going, Dave?" I asked.

"Not bad, not bad!" he said. I was looking around, afraid to enquire about the well-being of my neighbors in the park. I started with Billy, the die-hard.

"How's Billy?" I asked.

"Oh, great, great," he said.

"And Timmy?" I asked.

"Ah shit, ah shit, ah shit, man. Timmy died last week. Had a seizure. His heart just exploded."

Thanksgiving in the Park

I don't know if I'll have the heart to do the turkey this year, although I know there will probably be someone looking forward to it. I'm grieving about Timmy, Maximilian, Bob, Lloyd and Jimbo. They've all been found dead in or around the park since the first time I cooked the Thanksgiving turkey.

Eviction

One day I looked out the window and saw my Italian neighbor crying on the street corner. It was bitterly cold and she was wearing only a housecoat and slippers. I hadn't seen her for two weeks, since I'd been traveling. She beckoned me to come down and I dashed across the street, barely avoiding the oncoming traffic. She was distraught.

"What's the matter?" I asked her as I slid my arm around her shoulder. She brushed me off.

"God forgive me," she said, "but I'm losing my religion because of this." She pointed to the pick-up truck parked in the alleyway, loaded with her belongings. "The building has been sold, and I've been evicted. I have until noon on Friday to get everything out."

I recalled a conversation we'd had a couple of months earlier. "I can't sleep at night," she told me. "I'm so nervous and worried all the time. I've been noticing a lot of people looking at the building I live in and I am afraid it will be sold. Nobody is saying anything and there are no 'For Sale' signs anywhere, but I have a terrible feeling. What will I do, where will I go if the building gets sold? Every morning of my life, I've gone to Mass at Sts. Peter and Paul down the street. I buy all my groceries in North Beach. This is where my life is. If I have to move, I won't be able to afford the rent in this neighborhood. What will I do in the suburbs?"

I'd told her "Try not to lose too much sleep over this. Don't let it make you sick. There are laws to protect you. You can't be evicted just like that."

About that time, I happened to be reading a book called *The End of Hidden Ireland* that gave recorded accounts of the eviction and forced emigration of the whole village of Ballykilcline in County Roscommon in l847. To show how poor these people were, a National School teacher in a neighboring community had taken an inventory of the possessions of the people in his area. Four thousand inhabitants in his parish, among them, owned 1 cart, 1 plough, 20 shovels, 32 rakes, 7 table forks, 93 chairs, 243 stools, 2 feather beds, 8 chaff beds, 3 turkeys, 27 geese, no bonnet, no clock, 3 watches and no looking glass above 3 pence in price.

Nearly 500 men, women and children were forced to walk the ninety miles from Ballykilcline to Dublin in treacherous weather and an even more treacherous political climate. On the road they encountered starving stragglers and exposed rotting corpses. All around, the air was filled with the stench of decaying potatoes. It took them four days and, someone figured, 140,000 footsteps each to get to the ferry in Dublin that would take them to the Liverpool docks. Because it was a forced emigration, they were "escorted" along the route. Their fate then depended on whether there was an "emigrant trade" boat in Liverpool to take them on the transatlantic journey to the New World.

They arrived in Liverpool, according to one witness, with "only the rags on their backs." Predators robbed them of their few possessions. If one member of a family was refused passage because of declining health or old age, the whole family would refuse to leave. They lived in holes and hovels in Liverpool, preferring to starve to death than to split up.

Of the 496 names that appeared on rent rolls in Ballykilcline only 298 of those names made it to Ellis Island in New York.

Eviction

My neighbor's plight saddened me. I would cry every time I saw her sitting by the window, wistfully watching the cable cars and the tourists go by.

Her worst fears came true, of course. The building was sold. I stood on the corner with her as her furniture was hauled away. She told me she was going to live with a relative in Vallejo and there was no room there for her belongings. She sold some of her furniture, but the load on the pick-up truck would be delivered to poor people.

We stood and watched the truck pull away from the curb. "Sixty-three years I've lived in this apartment" she said." Sixty-three years."

Poets Tell Our Stories

২০

I've been reading a slim volume of poetry titled *Dhar-makaya*, by Dublin poet Paula Meehan. Dharma is a Buddhist term meaning Light. I've marveled at how she turns the kind of urban poverty and deprivation of her childhood into beautiful poetry. The more I read, the more I wondered if she hadn't lived in my childhood home, perhaps as a sprite underneath the stairs or out the back yard in the coal shed, for in her writing she seems to be telling my story. Without ever meeting her, I feel her as a sister.

Meehan comes from the North side of Dublin, while I was born on the South side ten years earlier than she was. There has always been rivalry between the two sides of the River Liffey, the South believing itself more elite. And it was, if you didn't happen to look in the hidden alleyways and lanes sandwiched between rows of fancy Georgian houses on Merrion Square. My mother called the people who lived on the Square "the quality," implying that the rest of us were just the riff-raff.

As a child, Paula Meehan was shamed at school, just as I was. We were shamed for being poor and were often slapped and beaten, both in school and at home. There was no such thing as children's rights, and we had yet to learn about the politics of class.

Paula Meehan writes about the box room, the coal shed in the back yard, her mother's grave, and her father's swollen hands from plucking turkeys fourteen hours a day. I'm struck by how far we've come from there to here, this poet I'm so enthralled with and I. It's a long journey from where we were—spiritually, emotionally, psychologically and psychically battered—to a place where it's possible to shine a light into the dark corners of the past and see the rose growing out of the dirt.

I take comfort in her poetry. It's like a salve for my wounds. Paula Meehan's poems are beautiful odes to the touchy subject of urban poverty, deprivation and trauma. Poets tell our stories. They talk to us when we almost can't bear to hear our lives being told.

Forgiveness

Plum Village near Bordeaux is a community of Vietnamese monks and nuns started by the Rev. Thich Nhat Hanh, who was a delegate to the Paris Peace Talks in 1968 and now lives in exile in France.

I spent a couple of weeks there in community with peace activists from all around the world. Among those present were Americans who had fought in the Vietnam War, and some of whom were struggling to reconcile and forgive themselves for their deeds in combat. I also met a gentle monk named Benito there. He and I became fast friends from the moment we first met under a linden tree on the property. I promised that one day I would visit his pagoda outside Hanoi.

Several years later, I made good on my promise to visit Benito in Hanoi. My husband and I traveled by plane, bicycle, boat and train from one end of Vietnam to the other. We talked to a lot of people. Whenever I brought up the subject of war, it seemed to fall on deaf ears—and everyone expressed interest in meeting more people from the United States so they could get to know them.

I asked Minh, a young woman I met, "How come the Vietnamese have forgiven the Americans for the War?"

"Because eighty percent of the Vietnamese are Buddhists," she answered. "It is easy for them to forgive."

When I met up with Benito, he drove me around Hanoi on the back of his moped. In the countryside, we borrowed bicycles and rode alongside the rice paddies. It was one of the most peaceful times of my life.

When I returned to San Francisco, I told my friend Lee Thorn about Benito. Lee, a Vietnam veteran involved with Veterans for Peace, frequently takes aid and medical supplies to Laos. On his next trip to Asia, Lee visited Vietnam for the first time since the war. I arranged for Benito to pick him up at the train station in Hanoi. They had fought on opposite sides in the war and there was a kind of reconciliation. It was the beginning of a significant friendship and alliance.

Shortly after my visit to Vietnam, a Buddhist group in Colorado invited Benito to the U.S. After some difficulty, Benito finally got his visa and stayed with me in San Francisco for four and a half months. He sent out a call through Lee Thorn and Veterans for Peace that he would lead a daily walking meditation around City Hall, and he met many vets this way. Benito went to an ecumenical conference here and was invited to go to Mozambique to start a Buddhist community there.

I heard from him a couple of times, and then lost touch. I have been unable to get any news of him either through friends traveling to Vietnam or from calling his pagoda in Hanoi. But then, I have to remember that Buddhists live in the present moment.

A Loving Woman

જી

I first met Mary Whooley in 1980 when I was organizing an event to celebrate the 100th anniversary of the birth of Irish playwright Sean O'Casey. And like most new arrivals from Ireland, I found my way to the Irish Castle Shop on Geary Boulevard, which she owned.

I was amused when Mary pulled me close and whispered very softly in my ear, "O'Casey was a bit of a Socialist, wasn't he?" I didn't know whether she thought that was a good or a bad thing, but it enamored me of Mary for life.

She was a native of Donegal and in her youth she'd thought she had the vocation to be a nun—but when she joined the convent, she realized the very next morning that she'd made a big mistake and left soon after that. As a girl, she had sung in a trio with her two sisters and all of them had been accomplished musicians. When Mary moved to San Francisco, she married John Whooley and together they had five children. Before Mary opened the Irish Castle Shop, she gave piano lessons at her home.

After a few visits to her shop, I could see it was a haven for people from all walks of life, the famous and the infamous alike. It was a place where Irish and non-Irish went for a chat and a bit of comfort. Any time I went in there, there'd be people gathered around the counter—a mix of tourists who had come in to browse and a person or two from the Irish community who just dropped by to talk. I ran into Sinéad O'Connor there one day when she was in town for a gig. Mary made her a cup of tea.

Mary had the warmest way about her. When people left the shop, they felt they'd made a new best friend, for Mary was a marvelous listener and was genuinely interested in people and their stories. She loved truth and honesty and saw beauty in every living thing.

Mary would call me up regularly to tell me how much she appreciated the truth in some newspaper column I'd written for the *Irish Herald*. She thanked me for writing about subjects she felt others were afraid to touch. "You keep the Irish honest," she told me once. She was my champion, always there with encouragement.

When I was diagnosed with breast cancer several years ago, she was there to comfort and support me through the ordeal. After that it wasn't long before she was diagnosed herself with stage four breast cancer.

Mary did all the things she was told to do. She had invasive surgery, underwent some heavy-duty chemotherapy and then had radiation treatments. Through it all, she tried to keep the shop open for all the weary travelers who dropped by. After putting up a valiant fight, Mary was finally told that the cancer had spread to her liver and bones.

I went to see her at the hospital and she told me she'd accepted the fact that she would soon die, that she was ready. She confided that she might have a buyer for the Irish Castle Shop, someone from Donegal. She said she would like the shop to remain as a sanctuary for those who needed it.

"The hardest part about dying," she said, "is leaving my grandchildren."

Mary died at home, surrounded by her children and grandchildren, and was buried on the 16th of April, the day of the full moon. At the funeral mass at St. Dominic's Church, her children paid tribute to their mother. I was deeply moved, listening to their remarks, because they expressed her essence and her worth.

She shines through them today. Beautiful singers and musicians all, they sang and played during the service. A rainbow of grandchildren, husbands, boyfriends and girlfriends filled the front pews of the church. Mary's two sisters gave a glorious rendition of "O Sanctissima" and a friend read from the *Song of Songs*.

Paddy's Day

Paddy was my brother Sean's closest friend. When I first started hearing about him, he had worked as a ship's radio operator and everybody knew him as Paddy the Sailor. He was as well-loved as anyone I have ever known.

When he was not at sea, Paddy could always be found on a barstool in McDaid's pub in Dublin. In looks and intensity, Paddy was like the actor Ed Harris. He had those same twinkly blue eyes with something steely under the surface that made you careful not to take a joke too far.

Life was going along swimmingly for Paddy. He had the great big ocean to sail on and a barstool when he was on leave. Not a soul believed that Paddy would ever do anything different, but one day everything changed. Into McDaid's walked a New York Irish woman who sat herself down on the stool next to his and the rest, as they say, is history.

He and Trish got married, settled in New York City and had a family. Paddy continued on with the high seas and the drinking as usual. But then I heard through the grapevine that his wife had given him an ultimatum. She wanted him on shore and sober. He quit the sea first and later swore off the booze and started working on construction sites.

One year Paddy told me he had taken up cycling and was fiercely devoted to it. Next thing I heard, he was going to ride in the Tour de France. I happened to be in France on the day the race finished and will never forget the joyful, smiling man who looked for me in the bleachers at the finish line on the Champs Elysees in

Paris. I have a picture etched in my mind of that gloriously warm day and the pride of achievement that shone on Paddy's face. From then on, I retired "Paddy the Sailor" and began referring to him as "Paddy the Biker."

Next time I heard about him was in a phone call from my brother Sean, who was with him in New York. "Paddy is not doing well," he told me. The first sign of trouble was when he blacked out and fell off his bike. "He has malignant brain tumors and the prognosis is not good." In the months that followed, the hell of chemotherapy took its toll and I was almost afraid to call, scared of hearing something terrible.

Then planning a trip to New York, I tried to contact Paddy. I phoned for several days, but there was no one home and no message on the answering machine. I feared the worst. In a couple of days, I got a call from Trish.

"Paddy is off cycling in Italy," she said. "A few of his mates came by one day and told him to pack the bike. They were taking him racing for ten days."

On the night he got back from Italy, Lew and I had fish and chips with him and Trish at O'Flanagan's pub in their neighborhood. He looked fit as a fiddle, although he was bald and had some scars on his skull to show for his medical troubles. He was exhilarated as he described riding his bike up the hills in the Dolomites, sometimes passing twenty-five-year-old racers as he went.

"How can you be this fit after all you've been through in the past year?" I asked him. He described his months in bed when, zapped from chemo, he would get up whenever he had a teensy weensy bit of energy and ride the stationary bike that he kept in his bedroom.

He looked so relaxed and happy. The flinty tension of "Paddy the Sailor" was gone and a mellower "Paddy the Biker" talked lovingly of his relationship with his two kids and how wonderful everything was between him and Trish. He was holding her hand when he said, "No more doctors and hospitals for me. I just want to live my life."

Trish touched his knee under the table and with tears in her eyes said, "I respect his decision. What else can I do?"

Singing for Mandela

ℰ

I remember well the day Nelson Mandela was released from prison. Aisling, Lew and I were driving back from Mt. Tamalpais when we heard the news on the radio. It was an emotional moment for all of us.

Aisling was a teenager by this time and had been acting out and hanging out in all kinds of dangerous ways. She'd use a ladder and climb out the window late at night to join her friends. (Does this sound familiar?) We'd have to go looking for her at midnight down at Sixth and Market where she and her girlfriend Meeka would try to pass themselves off as older, so they could get in to see *The Rocky Horror Picture Show*. On the weekends she would perform with a hip-hop band at clubs in Oakland, staying out way past her curfew. She'd been doing this since she was twelve or thirteen. Lew and I were frustrated beyond description with her at this point.

Aisling and I had been in the choir Vukani Mawethu ("People Arise" in Swahili), formed in 1986. We sang songs in Swahili, Zulu and Xhosa, at demonstrations, university campuses and on the docks of Oakland and San Francisco where the International Longshore and Warehouse Union (the ILWU, Lew's union) was refusing to let cargo from South Africa in or out.

When we heard about Mandela's release we opened the car windows, and sang at the top of our lungs "Nkosi Sikelel iAfrika" which was the anthem of the African National Congress, Mandela's party, and is now South Africa's National Anthem.

That was when Aisling announced she had something she wanted to say to us. She told us how much she loved and respected us. She was, she said, overwhelmed with gratitude for the values we had taught her. She said, thanks to the way we'd raised her, this was a day that was full of meaning and hope.

As she spoke, I could hear my heart pumping faster. I remember the fierce love I felt for her.

Part 6
Thoughts

❧

Daydreams don't have to be about faraway places. For me, they can be about anything from the corns on my feet to international affairs, from taking out the trash to dealing with breast cancer. The gift is that I've learned to listen to my own thoughts. I kept a diary when I was going through breast cancer and turned my thoughts into a monologue with songs that I perform for doctors, nurses and cancer patients.

Living with Cancer

There were three auld gypsies came to our hall door.
They came brave and boldly, O
And there's one sang high and the other sang low
And the lady sang The Raggle Taggle Gypsy O.
She gave to them a glass of wine.
She gave to them some brandy O
And the fine gold ring that the lady wore
She gave it to the raggle taggle gypsy O.

When I was in school, I used to tell stories, recite poems and sing songs about the history and folklore of Ireland. I won prizes and got my picture in the paper. It was great. Most Irish people will sing for you at the drop of a hat. But there was a time when I didn't feel much like singing—the time I thought I might be facing death.

It was November 1994, five o'clock in the morning and I was sitting in my kitchen feeling so lonely. I had a lot on my mind and couldn't sleep. Lew and Aisling were still in bed. I switched on the radio and heard Van Morrison singing "You Don't Pull No Punches But You Don't Push the River" from *Veedon Fleece*. Those words kept repeating over and over. Maybe that's why I was up so early. Maybe I needed to hear that.

I love music. It pulses the blood in my veins and I always have a song going round in my head. I also have a soft spot for Van Morrison, probably because we are the same age and were both born in Ireland. I can relate to everything he sings. And now here he was, in the middle of the night, coming to me over the airwaves singing "You Don't Pull No Punches But You Don't Push the River." The way I heard it, the message was, "Just sit in the shit, this, too, shall pass."

The day before had been my mother's birthday and the anniversary of my father's burial. It was a strange kind of day to get the news that I had breast cancer. The cancer was in the lower part of my left breast, near my heart.

When you get diagnosed with a life-threatening illness, you can drive yourself nutty trying to figure out the reason why. Could it have been all those years of longing for my father's love? Those years of mothering my six younger brothers and sisters and all the birds with the broken wings that I brought home along the way? And then there was my best friend Gene and all those young men with AIDS that I had sat with during their dying moments. Were there too many people dependent on this breast, this heart? I'd been a political activist since I was eleven years old, and always seemed to have an antenna that tapped into people's pain. The whole world and his wife felt at liberty to tell me their troubles. Could taking on the pain of the world create a disturbance that started the cancer?

I had been on an emotional roller-coaster ever since I'd found a lump in my breast. The hospital lost the first biopsy, and I didn't find out for ten days that they had lost it. Then they did a second one. I waited and waited, and when I finally phoned the hospital for the results, they said, "You'd better come in right away."

Thank God my husband came with me, because when I heard the words "breast cancer" I went into the twilight zone. I stopped hearing. I stopped feeling. When I finally spoke, I said, "Doctor, tell me how long I can live without getting treatment. I'm not afraid to die. I've seen death up close and it doesn't scare me, but please, please, please, do not tell me that I have to have chemotherapy." Then this little girl voice came out from somewhere deep down inside me and said, "Doctor, will I lose my hair?"

In my research, I learned that the drug most prescribed to women with breast cancer is made by a pesticide manufacturer. I wanted to get up on my soap box about the government not holding big corporations accountable for pollution, about how their greed is killing our planet—and me—for profit! There are hormones in the meat, pesticides on the fruit and vegetables. There are dyes on all our food to make it look more appealing so that we'll buy more, spend more, eat more. My body had just caved in under the stress of it all. (My daughter once said to me when I was raving, "Mom, you're up on your soap dish again.")

I asked myself, "Had I stayed in Ireland, would I have gotten breast cancer?" No one in my family ever had cancer, as far as I know. I wasn't a candidate for breast cancer. There was no family history. I was under fifty and I'd had my children when I was young. I didn't drink or smoke.

After doing a lot more research, I was too scared not to have surgery. I knew that in the end, I would do whatever I could to *live*. On the 12th day of the 12th month—12 is my lucky number—I had a lumpectomy. They cut off only part of the breast. Then they removed nineteen lymph nodes to see if the cancer had traveled.

It was drive-in surgery. They kicked me out of hospital right after the operation with tubes sticking out of me and little bottles strapped to my chest to catch the blood. I should have been kept in hospital. I was so sick I couldn't even keep water down. I would go in and out of consciousness with my darling Lew there beside me, trying so hard not to show his pain and anguish. My friend Barbara Clarke would come by to relieve him and climb into bed beside me and hold me and just *be there*. Once I woke up to find my good friend Dennis sitting in an armchair at the foot of the bed keeping vigil, and every few days Marilyn came by with cauldrons of matzo ball soup. I couldn't have pulled through without the rallying round of my family and friends. I truly felt loved.

After the surgery, I had four rounds of chemotherapy and thirty-five radiation treatments. Nothing could have prepared me for the nightmare of chemotherapy. There were days of intense nausea and disorientation. I was so wired I couldn't sleep and when I did fall asleep, I had dark, dark dreams. There were excruciating headaches, blackouts and occasional blindness. I had visions of slashing my wrists or driving that $50 carving knife I'd just bought through my heart—but I didn't even have enough coordination to hold my knitting needles steady. There were days when I would have welcomed death.

I also had acupuncture and Reiki. I cooked Chinese herbs when I could stomach it, and drank Kombucha tea. I went to support groups. I prayed and meditated. I talked to a lot of people and I read a lot. I read again and again that people with a good attitude survive longer. I tried very hard to have a good attitude, but it wasn't easy.

People empathized and said they were sorry. "If anyone can do it with grace, you can, Renée," they told me. As if grace had anything to do with it. I was the only one who knew what it was like. I was the one going through the fire. There were days when I was sick and tired of being "good old Renée." I wanted to scream, "What about me? It's my turn! I'm not everyone's fucking mother!"

I'd been doing Tai Chi in the park every morning for ten years. One morning I was sitting in my favorite spot under some beautiful trees, breathing in their oxygen. The sun rose over the tops of the buildings and bathed me in golden light.

Breathing in I calm myself.
Breathing out I smile.
I dwell in the present moment.
This is a wonderful moment.

I looked up at my favorite tree in all her winter bareness and I thought if that tree—Hazel, I called her—can look that majestic and powerful, then so can I. I took inspiration from Hazel and decided then and there that I would shave my head. I couldn't believe how attached I was to my hair. I had big hair. I knew I would lose it to the chemotherapy drugs, but I wanted to do it myself. I didn't want to wake one morning and find it all on the pillow beside me—or worse yet, see it flying out the window of the MUNI bus.

On a rainy Sunday morning, nine women gathered at my apartment to shave my head. We ranged in age from twenty to seventy. There was no grand plan or agenda; we just wanted to create a women's day together. Each woman instinctively brought something that had special meaning to her. Barbara brought a ceramic statue, The Blue Goddess she called it. Other women brought a carved sandalwood Buddha; a photo of an Indian holy woman, Ammaji, in a gorgeous red sari; and a picture of our Lady of Guadalupe in her mantle of blue, covered over with stars and festooned with roses. There was a hand-beaded peace pipe with an eagle's feather dangling from it, and a talking stick, candles, flowers, incense and all kinds of crystals. Believe me, I was taking everything I could get. I had atheists, animists, Christians, Muslims and Jews on three continents praying for me.

We created an altar on the coffee table and I lit a fire in the fireplace. My daughter Aisling, who was twenty years old at the time, started us off by singing:

Why should I feel discouraged?
Why should the shadows come?
Why should my heart feel lonely
And long for heaven and home
When Jesus is my portion
A constant friend is He.
His eye is on the sparrow
And I know He watches over me.

I was so touched by that. I really wanted to let it in, to believe that somewhere, somehow, I was being taken care of.

Something wonderful happens when women gather together, particularly around a fire. Fire is such a primal thing. These women didn't all know one another, but their power in the circle was awesome. They gave loving, spontaneous outpourings as each person said how she had met me and what I meant to her in her life. Each sang a song or read a poem or shared something authentic.

Rachelle said she was angry at the injustice of it all, and only wanted to scream. I handed her a pillow and she sobbed and screamed into it. Patty led us in a visualization. We imagined all the cancer cells rising up into my hair before we cut it off. Cutting the hair was a lot of fun. Because Rachelle is a professional hair dresser, each cut created some new look or style. The metamorphosis was slow and it was intriguing to see all the different Renées come and go. Aisling gave me the final shave and this bald goddess emerged. April sprinkled my head with angel dust and put on a crown she had made for me.

We placed all the hair into a ceramic bowl and took turns throwing handfuls into the blazing fire. I played a tape of Robbie Robertson's "Music for The Native Americans" and we grabbed anything we could find that would make noise: a tambourine, a drum, a rain stick, some cymbals and maracas. We danced and sang and chanted and got as goofy as we wanted. When we were tired out, we sat around the fire eating the bagels and cream cheese that Marilyn had brought and reading aloud from a book of politically correct fairy stories.

Late in the evening, the head-shaving party broke up. I couldn't wait to go outside and show off my new look. It was raining, but I didn't care. I put on my coat and walked out baldheaded into the cool grey San Francisco night.

Chemotherapy is not like a toothache or giving birth. *You don't forget it.* One of the side effects is a heightened sense of smell. I could vomit if my husband opened a can of cat food three rooms away. I was lying on the couch one morning in the horrors of chemo, getting ready to weep over some tiny little thing, when I smelled roses. I knew I didn't have roses in the house, so I went looking to find where the perfume was. I followed my nose to a bookshelf in the dining room. A lot of junk had fallen down behind it, so I got a broom handle and dragged it all out. One item was a card with some dried rose petals inside from my friend Gene. He'd died suddenly of AIDS six years earlier, but in my chemotherapy haze I could smell the roses he had given me— dry as they were—as vibrant, living flowers. The card said, "Your friend in body and soul, Gene."

We never know when our friendship, or maybe just some little thing we say, will change someone's life. I'd met Gene when we were singing together at an anti-apartheid rally in Oakland with the Freedom Song Network. He was one of the most talented people I'd ever known. He was an actor, singer, painter and sculptor. And he was a marvelous cook. He pushed me to do more of the creative things I loved to do but felt insecure about.

When I felt well enough, I wrote an article about AIDS in memory of Gene and sent it out thinking, "What the hell? There's nothing to lose here." Much to my surprise, a couple of major newspapers picked it up. That led to a job writing a monthly column for the *Irish Herald*. The following year, I formed an acting group, James Joyce's Women, to perform Joyce's stories. Over the past few years I've had a fun job at the box office of *Beach Blanket Babylon*—a legendary North Beach theatrical extravaganza—where I got to be around a lot of creative people.

Finding Gene's card with the dried roses set in motion a chain of events that made my life richer. It brought home to me how precious and how uncertain life is, and also how short it can be. One of his greatest gifts to me arrived long after he had gone.

There's something in that song, "The Raggle Taggle Gypsy." The story within it is about a woman getting a wake-up call that takes her away from her old life and starts her on a new course. She was married to a fine lord with land and riches, but once she expressed herself singing and traveling with the gypsies, there was no going back. Her husband came home one night and the servants told him, "The lady's away with the gypsies, Sir." So he saddled up his milk-white steed and rode all over the countryside searching for his darling, but she wouldn't go back.

Living with Cancer

Yerra what do I care for a fine feather bed?
What do I care for blankets O?
Tonight I'll lie in the wide-open fields
In the arms of my raggle taggle gypsy O.
For you rode east when I rode west.
You rode high when I rode low.
I'd rather have a kiss from the yellow gypsy's lips
Than all of your gold and silver O!

If the Shoe Fits

༢

The ad in the Sunday newspaper said they were looking for people who suffered from corns, bunions or calluses caused by wearing high-heeled shoes. I phoned the 800 number and was asked some personal questions about my feet. The woman told me I qualified to participate in a study that involved talking about my corns for fifteen minutes.

I immediately flashed back to my first pair of high heels when I was sixteen. I had just walked out the front door when a neighbor, looking up at me towering over him, announced, "You should never wear high heels. You're too tall for them." It was just the kind of encouragement I needed to keep me in high heels for the rest of my natural life. I'm stubborn like that. I've fished in them, hiked in them and walked many a mile in them.

Once I went camping in Morocco in my favorite pair. When the heels wore down, I left them at the edge of the Sahara and hoped a Berber or Bedouin woman would pick them up on her nomadic wanderings and get a few more years' wear out of them.

When I first started wearing high heels, I used to buy them at a shop called Heathers on the quays in Dublin. Heathers had thousands of shoes, and sold them at huge discounts. The problem at the time was, Heathers rarely had a left and right shoe the same size, with the same appearance, that went together to form a pair. You would have to rummage through all the boxes and try to invent a pair. I remember one time buying a beautiful "pair" with the left foot a half size bigger than the right foot. Another time, I found two red ones—a left and a right in the same size, but two different colors of red. I polished them within an inch of their lives to make the reds match.

When I was old enough to earn a living and buy my own shoes, I had to have the most gorgeous and unusual shoes imaginable. I became known for my fabulous shoes. Italian ones were my first choice, with French a close second. I have to admit that in recent years I have gotten more sensible concerning the comfort of my shoes, but they still have to be unusual and beautiful. I still like to shop for a bargain, but there has to be a left and a right shoe in the same size and color. That is my bottom line.

When the day arrived for the fifteen-minute interview, I pondered what shoes to wear. Would it be the black suede ankle boots with the rhinestone Eiffel Towers on the heels, or the crushed velvet high top shoes with the wide satin ribbons? Decisions, decisions, decisions. When I got there, I was relieved to find that it was a woman who would talk to me about my feet. I knew she could relate as she took photos of my corns and I told her of the adventures that had caused them. When we finished, she handed me a check and a supply of some newfangled corn pads.

As I walked the mile and a half home in my high heels, I fantasized about a possible new career, asking myself, "Could all that money I spent on high heels finally pay off?"

Delusion

ఌ

I haven't been obsessed with my weight since I sold my full-length mirror in a garage sale. The last time I thought about it was when I was on vacation with Lew. We were getting ready for a late night dinner in Barcelona and I decided to wear some black pants I had purchased a couple of months earlier. I had saved them for the trip and planned to wear them with something flimsy and lacy. When I put them on, I was astounded. The pants were huge on me. I tried to intrigue my husband with what I termed "a miracle."

"Can you believe this?" I asked him excitedly. "It looks like I've lost fifteen or twenty pounds, without even trying."

I was on a natural high, whistling "Lady of Spain" as I got dressed. I kept giggling at the good fortune that allowed me to drop two dress sizes in two months without dieting, and indulged in whatever food I desired at dinner that night. We stayed up later than usual because I wanted to promenade in my new incarnation as the Queen of Sheba. My husband was on a contact high, perhaps mirroring my feelings of being "arm candy" or a "trophy wife."

Getting ready for bed, I opened the closet to hang up my clothes and saw the black pants hanging there. "What's going on here" I said aloud. "How can I be wearing them and have them hanging in the closet at the same time?" I stepped out of the ones in which I had sashayed around all evening and examined them closely. "Waist 36 inches" was written on the inside label.

I had been wearing my husband's trousers.

Talking Trash

꿔

On a walk in my neighborhood, I counted four couches with "Free" signs on them. I wondered if their owners were moving, or if perhaps there was a great sale on sofas somewhere. A few days later, on a different block, I saw a baby's cradle and a chest of drawers. Normally, I'd stop and examine the stuff. I've brought home a few treasures that way. But I've changed my ways.

I had to curtail my collecting when two people had wheezing attacks at my place. Both were allergic to cat hair and dust mites. I have two hairy cats and armadas of dust-gathering objects: books, swan and elephant figurines, a perfume bottle collection, bead and fabric collections and twenty pairs of shoes. Not to mention the clothes, which are everywhere. I don't have enough closet space for two reasons. One, I live in a hundred-year-old building. Two, I have a lot of clothes.

The clothes-collecting is a throwback to my days of living in poverty. How can I forget all those shame-filled times when I had to wear other people's clothes? I often had clothes from older people that were completely inappropriate for my age. I remember a suit that my teacher, Miss Garrick, gave me when I was fifteen years old. It was very much like the suit Jimmy Stewart bought for Kim Novak in the film *Vertigo*: fitted in all the right places. I can still feel my mortification at being whistled at when I wore it.

My friends' refusal to come to my dusty, hairy apartment annoyed me. In a fit of pique, I resolved to do some spring cleaning. I plugged in the vacuum cleaner, thinking the rugs might be a good place to start. The vacuum belched out toxic-smelling black fumes. I had to open all the windows. I tied a scarf around my mouth so I wouldn't choke. When I threw a glass of water on the thing while it was still plugged in, I knew I had lost my mind. I put the vacuum out on the sidewalk and did the only thing I could. I made a cup of tea..

A few days later, I received information in the mail about a seminar called "Letting Go of Clutter." I signed up.

"What is your first memory of collecting?" the teacher asked the group.

"I started collecting things after my mother gave away my electric train to a boy cousin without asking me," one woman explained. "Now even my bathtub has stuff stored in it. I had to join a gym so I can take a shower."

"Oh, that's not the worst I've heard," said the teacher. "I had a client whose garage was so full he started storing things in his car. When his car was full, he started driving a rental car."

I began to wonder what I was doing there. Most of the clutterers were afflicted with psychological scars from dark childhood memories. My problem was that, growing up, I was never taught to keep tidy. Getting the next meal was the only thing that mattered in our household.

The teacher advised us to start by picking up and cleaning one small area, and to commit at least two hours to the task. I took her advice, but after seven hours of work, I was still looking at the same awful chaos that had devastated me before I took the clutter seminar.

I have to confess, there are some things I am incapable of throwing out. I still have the black crochet skirt I bought in Camden Town in London in 1964. Then there's the bias-cut skirt I was wearing the day I became pregnant with my daughter Aisling. Of course, I couldn't possibly part with my mother's apple green 1940s swing coat that still has a lemon drop—her favorite kind of sweets—in the pocket. And I'll never give up the blue silk caftan with the orange hand-painted fish given to me by my youngest sister, Veronica.

I was sitting in the middle of the chaos, trying not to cry, when my friend Dierdre arrived unannounced, bearing sweets. We had some tea and cakes and I told her my troubles. She confided that she had clutter issues as well and offered to help me clean up the mess. When we were carrying the bags of trash outside to the sidewalk, she said, "I've got to get rid of some of my own clutter. I've been meaning to throw these away for years."

She took off her shoes and dumped them on top of the pile.

Cats Are Our Companions

Cats live easily with humans, yet still retain some of their wild qualities. For thousands of years, they were worshipped as gods in Egypt. In Europe during the Dark Ages, at the time of the Inquisition, cats were seen as the embodiment of the devil and were burned alive. It seems we either love them or we hate them.

My experience with cats came through my daughter, Aisling. From the time she was very little, she would beg me to get her a pet. We've always lived in rented apartments with "No Pets" policies, and the best I could do for my daughter was to buy her some birds. We started out with two finches, and before long the family of birds grew to nine. Still, it wasn't enough for her. She brought home garden snails one time and kept them in a box until they disintegrated, which was only a matter of days. All animals seemed to take to her. This became clear the day I saw her stoop down and pick up a pigeon in Washington Square Park. Another time when we were out camping, I freaked out when I caught her feeding a raccoon.

What she wanted most of all was a "real pet," which in her parlance meant a dog or a cat. She made several attempts to sneak kittens into the house, but I always insisted she take them back to the people who gave them to her. I still feel guilty about that, for I hadn't yet learned what a wonderful companion an animal can be. When Aisling turned fourteen, I relented and told her she could have a cat because I believed she was old enough to be responsible for one.

We went to the SPCA and a very shy, docile cat approached us and looked at us soulfully. The information about the cat said that she was about three years old and had been adopted and returned three times because she was a "scaredy-cat." She would hide in a closet or under a bed and refuse to be coaxed out. The worker at the shelter told us the cat had been abused and advised us to think long and hard before choosing her from among all the cats available for adoption. Aisling turned to me and said, "Mom, we have to get her. She looks just like you." That was the deciding factor and we brought the frightened animal home with us.

Being a musical child, Aisling named the cat Tila for the musical notes "ti" and "la"—as in "do, ti, la, so." It took a bit of time, but Tila eventually settled in with our family. One of the ways Tila had been abused was that her claws had been removed. De-clawing is painful in more ways than one. Imagine having all the joints in your fingers broken deliberately. That's what it is like, and it leaves a cat with no defense mechanism. It also deprives the animal of the ability to scratch, an integral part of cat behavior. I learned that one reason cats scratch is to release endorphins in the brain. These endorphins have a calming effect, and are basically kitty stress-relief.

At first, everything frightened Tila. We lavished her with love and after a while Aisling brought home a brand new kitten for companionship for Tila. Omar had just been weaned from his mother and persisted with Tila until she let him "nurse." It seemed to us that both cats got a lot out of it. Omar got no milk, of course, but much comfort.

Tila is nineteen years old, and she and her pal Omar have lived happy and serene lives. Now Tila is dying. She has not eaten for two weeks and has not had water for four or five days. She stays in close proximity to us humans, not hiding under the bed or crouching in closets. At night we sit in the kitchen for hours in the darkness, listening quietly to classical music. Tila sits on a cushion with a hot-water bottle underneath, Omar gazes out wistfully at the moon.

Some well-meaning friends have advised me to take Tila to Animal Control and "have her put down," but they don't know her like I do. In the natural world animals get old and die naturally. Tila's life is very close to its end. For the next day or two, her human family and Omar, her feline friend, will keep her company as she prepares for her leave-taking.

Hugging is Good for You

୧

My friend, Barbara Clarke, who is a midwife in New Mexico, sent me an email about twins who'd been born prematurely. They were placed in separate incubators because one was healthier than the other and was expected to live, while the other looked like she wouldn't make it. A nurse in the facility fought to have both of them placed in the same incubator. Almost immediately, the stronger of the two put her arm across the body of the sickly one—whose vital signs improved right away.

This corroborates what scientists have been saying for years, that being touched can make us feel better and in some cases even give us a longer lease on life.

I once read a story about a woman referred to as The Hugging Saint from India. She is known simply as Amma or Mother, and travels around the world hugging people. She has hugged more than twenty million people.

Ammaji, as she is known, visits the U.S. twice a year, and I went to see her and get a hug. I was thrilled to be sitting next to Dr. Martin Luther King Jr.'s daughter, Yolanda. It's not easy to explain exactly what takes place when one gets a hug from Ammaji. In an interview, Yolanda King described it as "a divine spiritual energy. When Ammaji hugged me, I grasped for the first time the essence of true fulfillment and unconditional love. I felt like I was flying without wings." My own experience was that of disappearing and ceasing to be. Afterwards I felt a blissful peace.

Later on, another hug made me feel lucky to be alive. I was in the middle of treatment for breast cancer, bald from chemotherapy, raw from radiation and exhausted because my immune system was shot. I was barely holding back the tears when I stepped on the crowded elevator at Kaiser Hospital. Suddenly, I noticed a very tall, very thin man at the back wearing a large button that said "I GIVE HUGS."

I looked over the heads of the other people in the elevator and asked, "Do you give them to strangers?" He stepped forward and held me in a warm embrace. When we reached the lobby and the doors opened, we said, "Thank you" to each other and went our separate ways.

The Dearly Departed

∽

When my friend Dennis lost his brother, he began speculating about the possibility of communicating with him "on some other frequency," as he called it. His parents were already dead and his brother Fred was his only sibling. The brothers were as different as chalk and cheese. Dennis mourned that they had never become great friends, but they loved each other even though they had many philosophical differences.

Dennis healed his emotional wounds by putting together a book of photos and stories about Fred. He started working on a quilt that depicted his brother as an infant, asleep at the foot of their family tree. That was his way of communicating on another frequency.

British journalist, Justine Picardie, wrote in *Granta* magazine about the death of her sister, Ruth, from cancer at the age of thirty-three. After Ruth's diagnosis, the sisters promised always to talk to each other—even after death. In a dream, Justine saw Ruth with her hair dyed red.

"I thought you were dead," she said to her.

Ruth replied, "I've just gone to live in America."

Justine visited psychics, mediums, sensitives and intuitives in the hope of making contact with Ruth. One person she consulted claimed to have a means of recording the voices of the dead. She told Justine that the optimum time to set up a tape recorder was on the night of a full moon with a thunderstorm raging. It had something to do with electricity in the air.

When the elements were in her favor, Justine turned on the tape recorder and asked Ruth some questions. Her sorrow and grief were so great, and she wanted so desperately to hear her sister's voice, that when she played back the tape she was willing to believe the faint hiss of the tape recorder, probably her own breathing and the scratching of her chair against the wooden floor, was Ruth's almost inaudible voice.

The death of a loved one is never easy, no matter how many people we lose. For days after my father died, I had Technicolor dreams in which he was alive. I would ask him why he tricked me by pretending to die. He always had plausible answers. In one, he was a younger version of himself sporting an outrageous Mohawk hairdo. I loved those dreams; it was as if I had really visited him somewhere.

A couple of days after my father's funeral, I went to see a psychic in Dublin. I had heard marvelous reports from people who consulted her. I had never been to a psychic before and was curious. She was an unassuming woman living an unspectacular life in a modest home in an ordinary neighborhood. We made no small talk. I just sat down and she wrapped me in a blanket and told me to close my eyes.

"Who's the man who came in with you?" she asked.

"No one," I replied.

"It's your father. He has a bunch of lilacs for you." Lilacs are my favorite flower. "He says the hairdo was just a joke. There's a woman named Catherine with him." His grandmother's name was Catherine, and she had raised him. "He says to tell you his death was a warm one and his mother came to help him across to the other side."

For over an hour she talked of events, some significant and others small, that only my father and I knew about. It was all quite chilling. My brain started to look for logic in the encounter, but I decided just to enjoy the comfort I was getting from her stories.

After the session, I wrote all the details I could remember in my diary. When I went home and shared them with my mother and brothers and sisters, they said almost in unison, "Ah, that's great news!"

We all have different ways of dealing with death and we all have stories we tell ourselves to ease the pain.

The Spiritual Center

As the year 2000 approached, people started asking one another, "Where are you going to be for the Millennium?"

I would say something like, "Oh, probably the Pyramids in Egypt." After all, we should choose a place that has some spiritual energy, right? Then I thought about Monte Alban in Oaxaca, Mexico. Why not? It was all fantasy anyway.

Finding a place with "spiritual energy" is a very personal and individual thing. Hordes of people made the pilgrimage to Jerusalem for the Millennium and I can understand why. I remember one of the most moving experiences of my life was a visit to the Wailing Wall in Jerusalem. I am not a Jew, but I went out of respect for their history and out of curiosity. When I stood beside the wall, I found myself weeping. Floods of images rushed into my head. It was as if I wept for everyone who had ever suffered, including myself. I felt all my troubles lifted. Afterwards I wished that every town and city in the world had some form of Wailing Wall.

So where would I be for the Millennium? Would I be in some "spiritual" place? As the big event approached, I saw a column in the *San Francisco Chronicle* by Brad Newsham, about his trip to India. On a quest for the spiritual center of the earth, he was informed it was San Francisco! When he asked what it meant for a place to be the spiritual center, he was told, "The place where new ideas meet the least resistance."

That's an inspired description of the City, if I ever heard one! Here I was, in the most spiritual place on earth all along.

Part 7
Home

❧

Growing up in Ireland, I was always longing for else-where. I still am, but now sometimes that "elsewhere" means the land of my birth, my home.

Goodbye to the Past

❦

"What is home without a mother?" It's a slogan you'd see often in Irish homes in the old days. I pondered that sentiment as I left my mother's house for the last time.

My mother had died the previous year and I'd come home to sell her house and say good-bye to a lifetime of memories, both good and bad. In many ways, it was like another death.

Though no one in the family had liked living in that house, it had become a sanctuary of sorts as we grew up and left home—and our mother was its heart. Whether her children were going through divorces, health crises or temporary homelessness, they could find refuge in that house. Even if our mother was vexed with us or we'd had a major falling out, there was always the understanding that her children and her children's children would find an open door.

Before I left it for the last time, I asked the local priest, Fr. Roy, to come bless the house and exorcise all its demons. They were in the years and years of wallpaper, every year a new pattern, layered one over the other. The upside-down roses, put up by a drunken neighbor who hung the paper for a cut rate. The mismatched tea kettles, half a teakettle at the edge of each roll. My father did that job himself when he was either drunk or angry or both, and failed to match the pattern.

God only knows what secrets the carpets held. There were years and years of carpets, one on top of the other, all bought from Gypsies, Travelers or Pakistani salesmen who came to the front door offering bargains.

Fr. Roy blessed the house in the four directions—very Druidic, I thought. We prayed for all of those who had inhabited the house and all those who would live in it in the future. Then I poured holy water down the drains to flush out the final badness.

It was impossible to find rest that last night in the house. I was sleeping on the floor of the "box room," so named because it's very small and could be used to store boxes, but some people also used it as a small child's bedroom. I was almost twelve when the family moved into that house. I'd been promised the box room because I was the oldest, but we had no bed for it. Besides, one person in one bed in one room was a luxury our family could not afford in those years.

I eventually got my box room and many dreams were dreamed and shattered within its walls. When I was sixteen, I'd saved some "runaway money" to get to Paris. One night, my father stole it from where I'd hidden it in the mattress. Once he got his hands on the money, there was no hope of getting it back. It was pissed away in a pub or went on the horses. My dreams of living in Paris had had to be put on hold.

I tossed and turned that whole last night in the house, watching flashbacks of my life play out as I waited for morning to come—and it came none too soon.

When the sun was finally up, my brother Patrick and I sat outside the house in a furniture moving van, waiting for the postman to arrive and hoping he had the lease for my brother's new abode. If that piece of paper didn't come, we had nowhere to go. We watched the postman riding toward us on his bike. Would he stop at number 8? My brother went out to meet him in the drizzly rain.

"Have you anything for me?" he asked the man. The postman handed him the lease.

Goodbye to the Past

We said good-bye to the McDonalds and the McGarrys, our neighbors of forty-eight years. We handed over the keys to a young couple and a toddler standing at the front door, smiling broadly. My brother and I fought back tears. We waved to the new owners and we all wished each other good-bye, good luck, God bless and all the best.

The house without my mother counted as nothing. All my grief was about the loss of my mother, my hero.

On Being Hospitable

❧

Christmas is probably the most important time of year to the Irish, although a party could break out on any day of the year. We are well known for our hospitality and our love of music and tradition, and Christmas is the time when these qualities unfurl and are displayed like banners. As we emigrated to every corner of the globe, we have taken with us our love of words, music, merriment and generosity.

As early as the 5th century A.D., the Brehon Laws of ancient Ireland ordered us to "entertain guests without question." The Brehon Laws were transcribed by Irish monks, who were also responsible for transcribing the whole of western literature during the Dark Ages.

So "entertaining" was a law. Through the ages, the Irish have kept their doors open, with cauldrons of food boiling on the hob at all times. The weary traveler would be given food, drink and a place to lay a tired head. There would be *ceoltoiri, amhrainaithe, seanchaithe* and *aithriseoiri* (singers and musicians, traditional storytellers and reciter/mimics) close at hand and likely amongst the travelers themselves.

To this day, one of the things visitors love most about Ireland is how the food, music, and "the *craic*," meaning fun/conversation/music, just seem to materialize out of thin air. Here we are, more than fifteen hundred years later, with an ingrained sense in our nature to be hospitable.

I spent a couple of months living in a cottage in the west of Ireland. On several occasions, strangers knocked at the door and invited themselves in. "Would you make me just half a cup of tea?" one asked. Another day I was visiting a neighbor when some campers knocked on the door and handed her a frying pan and some sausages and rashers to fry because they didn't have a stove in their tent. One must always have something "on the hob" to offer a stranger—at the very least a cup of tea and some homemade bread or scones.

Sweet Treats

❧

"Life is uncertain. Eat dessert first." I read that sign on some very dodgy-looking sweets at a roadside stand high in the Himalayas.

I could hardly wait to tell my friend Dierdre about it, because she is the only person I know who eats dessert first on a regular basis. Dierdre and I talk about food a lot. We've often discussed the Irish and how food is such an important feature in our lives. That's not to say that other nationalities aren't as obsessed with food as the Irish, but food issues are deeply imbedded in the psyche of every Irish person—and if truth be told, of all people of Irish ancestry. It's a throwback to the Great Hunger of almost two centuries past, when the starving populace ate grass and seaweed and the dirt off the ground as they struggled against death.

I think this throwback is one of the reasons I'll eat almost anything I'm offered except fish eyeballs and the webs of ducks' feet. I ate them once and that was enough. Otherwise, I'm game to try just about anything.

I'm thinking now of Halloween and the traditional food that goes along with "Samhain," as it was known before the rest of the world co-opted this pagan festival and turned it into the "business" of Halloween. Samhain was the day when the veil between worlds was at its thinnest. This allowed departed souls to come back and roam the earth for one night. It was also the pagan New Year.

The menu for Samhain in my youth was colcannon, from the Gaelic *"col ceann fionn"* meaning "head of white cabbage," and barm brack from the Gaelic "*bairin breac*," meaning "speckled loaf."

Colcannon is actually made with green curly kale, a winter vegetable and member of the cabbage family. You can find kale at the farmers' markets in any town. One thing to remember about the variety you find in America is to cook the dickens out of it to get it soft. Cut the stalks off first and cook for at least half an hour, then drain and chop it up as finely as possible. Boil some potatoes to go along with it and mash or whip the whole lot together with butter and milk. It helps to heat the milk, or better yet cream, so you don't end up with a lukewarm dinner. Make a mound of it on your plate and scoop out a well in the middle for extra butter. I like to chop some raw scallions or shallots into it as well. Forget about your cholesterol for one night.

The tradition is to put a plain gold ring, a sixpence, a thimble and a button into the colcannon. The person who finds the ring in his or her portion will be married within a year. The sixpence represents wealth for the recipient. The button means bachelorhood. The thimble means you'll remain a spinster. Each prize is wrapped separately in waxed paper and mashed into the colcannon. (If you serve this to children, make sure they find the prizes before they put it into their mouths.) Until recently, Halloween was a fast day in the Catholic Church, which meant you could eat no meat. Now, you can enjoy good Irish sausages with your colcannon.

We also had my mother's delicious pancakes at Samhain, made with fresh-squeezed lemon juice and sugar. If these had a name, I don't remember what it was. The pancakes were simple fare, but scrumptious nonetheless. They are easy enough to make from scratch, but a pancake mix will serve just as well. To get them nice and thin, just add more milk or water. My friend Dierdre, the one who eats dessert first and spells her name funny (most Irish people spell it "Deirdre"), puts the batter in the fridge for a while before she makes the pancakes. She learned that from her grandmother, and I can honestly say that Dierdre makes the best pancakes I've ever tasted. So make the pancakes nice and thin like crepes and squeeze some lemon juice on them and finish off with a dusting of sugar. Forget about the diet.

I don't tackle making a barm brack myself because I don't like baking; I leave it to people who do it well. My mother always told us never to bake when we were in a bad mood or had a bad attitude about it, because it would show in the results.

Lady Gregory, one of the founders of the Abbey Theatre, used to bake a big barm brack and bring it to the theatre for the actors on opening night. I believe this is her recipe, give it a try if you are having a party:

1 lb. sultanas

1 lb. raisins

1 lb. brown sugar

Soak the whole lot overnight in 3 cups of black tea. Use good Irish tea. Don't use Lipton's; it's too bitter.

The next day add to this:

1 lb. flour

3 eggs, beaten

3 teaspoons baking powder

3 teaspoons mixed spice

Use three 6-inch baking pans and bake at 325° for 90 minutes. Take them out and brush with honey, then put them back in the oven for a few minutes to create a glaze. Let them cool before eating.

The Old Bog Road

❧

"Give up yer oul dreams," the voices in my head were telling me as I rode the trains in Ireland this past spring. Those voices were a reaction to what I was seeing as I traveled through some of my favorite counties, especially Clare and Galway. The dreams I was being told to give up were fantasies of someday owning a field or a cottage in one of these formerly idyllic nooks. Everywhere I looked, in every direction, there was building going on. Areas that were once considered to be at the back of beyond were now being overrun with new homes.

When I got back to San Francisco, I phoned my friend Eamonn, another member of the Irish Diaspora, who lives in Toronto. I asked him what was happening to Ireland and ranted on about the unbelievably ugly new homes I had seen along the wee boreens in the countryside. They look ridiculous, I told him, standing alone with nary a tree or a hedge in sight. Everything green had been razed to make room for them. Why don't people just live in their old cottages and put up gigantic signs saying, "I, so and so, have gobs of money?" A big sign like that would be less damaging to the environment and less of an eyesore on the landscape.

"Did you know I grew up on *the* Old Bog Road?" Eamonn asked. He was referring to the famous ballad "The Old Bog Road" that goes:

My feet are here on Broadway this blessed harvest morn,
But O the ache that's in them for the spot where I was born.
My weary hands are blistered from work in cold and heat,

And O to swing a scythe today,
Thro' fields of Irish wheat.
Had I the chance to wander back, or own a king's abode,
'Tis soon I'd see the hawthorn tree by the old bog road.

I thought Eamonn was pulling my leg. "No, I'm dead serious," he said. He told me his family had lived there for generations and that a relative of his, Teresa Brayton, had written the ballad. "But you'd want to see the road now," he said. "Two of my cousins are building mansions along it as we speak."

"Exactly my point," I told him.

Living in the old Ireland was like living inside a picture postcard. It's a small island and most structures were proportionate to the landscape. Ireland's natural beauty has long been her main attraction, but now she is being ripped and torn and gouged, mile by terrible mile, all around the island as Ireland's short-lived economic prosperity, the Celtic Tiger, drove some people to the brink of insanity. There is no rhyme or reason to the building mania except as a vulgar show of wealth. Maybe it's a reaction to Ireland having always been such a poor country, and then getting rich. The attitude may be, "I have the money so I'll build whatever I damn well please."

The Celtic Tiger has quit roaring and has shown itself to be merely a Marmalade Cat as the banks go bust and people lose their homes. In 2000, Ireland found itself among the richest countries in Europe. By 2011, it was almost bankrupt.

On my most recent trip back, much had changed because of the economic bust. There was a sense of "We are all in this together" and "We'll come through it." People once more had time to bid each other the time of day, hang out, relax and have a few laughs. I felt a completely different vibe from the time when everything was about money and everyone was stressed out because of it.

Ireland will never go back to being the poor country it was when I was growing up—but hopefully, there will now be time to examine all the ways in which the boom could have been handled differently.

Some Mother's Son

᷉

After one of my visits with my mother, I phoned my friend Peg in Cobh, County Cork. She was spending two months as artist-in-resident at the Sirius Art Center, working on a photography exhibit of Irish holy wells. Peg had a free apartment in the art center, which overlooked the harbor. A school of dolphins was cavorting when I arrived after walking the short distance from the train.

I commented on the great acoustics in the place, and after dinner we traded *sean nos*, or old-style songs, back and forth until we ran out of words.

The next morning on the train back to Dublin, I sat across from a man who looked as if he wasn't "quite the full shilling." He was filthy and toothless and wearing a snot-covered coat. His nails were black and broken, and he fidgeted and picked at them constantly. He carried a plastic bag full of plastic bags. This man looked directly at me and said, "Mother's Day is comin' soon. 'Mother' is a word I never use."

"But you just used it," I said. "Why don't you use the word 'mother'?"

"Because I never knew one, never saw one, never had one," he replied. "You're a Yank, are ye?" he went on.

"I'm a Dubliner," I answered. "But nowadays I live in San Francisco."

"What's Carmel like in California?" he asked. "Is it a religious place?"

"Only if money is your God," I quipped.

"Ah, sure, I thought it had something to do with the Carmelite nuns," he said. "Wasn't Ronald Reagan the governor of California? What was he like?"

We talked for a couple of hours and he knew more about U.S. history and politics than your average American high school graduate. He talked about Marx and Engels, Judaism and exotic foods.

The train was full and passengers around us were turning their eyes to heaven, thinking they were showing solidarity with me. Because they were embarrassed and uneasy, they thought surely I must be, too. I did not return their looks. I was having a good time. The man was as harmless as a dove. I offered to buy him a cup of tea and a sandwich. "Ah! No, no, no thanks," he protested. I hoped I hadn't patronized him.

I didn't see him get off the train. I suspect the conductors let him ride free back and forth, back and forth in the warm compartment because it was very, very cold outside.

Out with the Snakes

St. Patrick was a gentleman
He came from decent people.

So goes a ballad that did the rounds of the pubs in Ireland a hundred years ago. I was checking out the words for a presentation to high school students in honor of St. Patrick's Day. I was going to intersperse my story with some songs, in hopes of holding their attention.

That's a trick I've learned from my granddaughter, Alanna. She loves it when I sing some parts of whatever story I'm telling her. I dream up the stories as I go along and always make sure she and her brother Ronnie are featured characters in some of them. The more fantastical the stories, the better they like them. I was the same way. My father told stories, but always with a humorous twist. He even twisted nursery rhymes. One of his favorites was:

Mary had a little lamb
His feet were black as soot
And everywhere that Mary went
His sooty foot he put.

So there I was, standing in front of the class ad-libbing about St. Patrick, who was not even an Irishman. He was a lad of eleven or twelve when he was captured in England and brought to Ireland as a slave. He worked as a shepherd for six years in the hills of County Antrim in the Northern part of Ireland. It was a very lonely life, and he escaped by stowing away on a boat carrying Irish wolfhounds to the European markets, where they fetched a pretty penny.

Patrick did not make his way back to Ireland until he was a grown man. He fasted for forty days and forty nights to prepare himself for the Herculean task of driving the snakes out of Ireland. This snake business may be purely symbolic, much like the snake in the Garden of Eden, because no self-respecting snake could tolerate the weather in Ireland. The real explanation of "driving the snakes out" may be that the Druids wore tattoos of serpents around their wrists, and Patrick wanted them to change their pagan ways. The Druids were bards and poets and were highly thought of as singers and story-tellers, magicians and fortune-tellers. They were considered to be the most just of men and were judges of private and public disputes. Patrick had to make them change—either by turning them into Christians or by getting rid of them entirely—or he never would have had the authority to establish Christianity and launch a golden era of literature and education.

History tells us that the Celts who lived in Ireland before the coming of Christianity were barbarians. At least that's what the historians called them—but the historians were Romans, and they were the Celts' most bitter enemies. The Celts were actually warriors and hunters who loved to drink. They were tall, pale-skinned people who wore their hair long and put limestone on it to make it whiter. They went naked into battle and their women went into battle with them. The women often settled disputes between the warring tribes. They were fearless people with an amazing faith in the survival of the soul after death.

Their idea of heaven was a Land of Wonders that was reached after a journey in a glass boat. Beyond the seas somewhere, there was a great transparent tower and beyond the tower, fertile plains covered with strange trees stretched away into the distance. Some of these trees had silver branches with golden apples on them, and when the apples touched each other they made such beautiful sounds that anyone within earshot immediately forgot their troubles. Rivers of wine flowed at the foot of the trees, while the rain falling from the sky soaked the earth with beer. Wild pigs foraging in the forests would come back to life immediately after being slaughtered, so that the banquet never ceased.

This is what Patrick was faced with when he came back to Ireland. The poor barbarians were forced to clean up their act. Patrick had lived amongst them and knew their ways and their language. Maybe it was not too much of a stretch for them to believe the Garden of Eden story and the use of the shamrock to explain Three Gods in One: the Father, the Son and The Holy Ghost. They already believed in an afterlife for the soul, so believing in the resurrection of the body might not have been too hard to swallow.

I was talking on and on about all this, and in the middle of my story the teacher left me alone in the room with the kids. No sooner had the teacher left than the kids started hitting each other and throwing stuff and swapping cards and whistling. I told them to stop. They didn't care. My God, my story had turned them into Hooligans.

Well, the teacher eventually came back and broke up the melee. And I was wishing I were a Druid so I could turn myself into a tree.

Final Thoughts of Home

҈

I've been around the world four times, living or sojourning in more than 150 countries. The resourcefulness I learned as a child helped me do my travelling with very little money. I worked in travel-related jobs, signed up for courier flights and became an expert in finding the best travel bargains in newspapers, magazines and on the Internet.

I've camped in the Sahara in Morocco with the snow-capped Atlas Mountains for a backdrop. I've traveled from Moscow to Beijing on the Trans-Siberian Railway and floated down the Mekong River in Laos. When I spent a month traveling alone around Egypt in my twenties, all my friends said I was mad—but not as mad as when I signed up to accompany a planeload of Irish soccer fans to the World Cup in Seville. I'll admit it was total chaos, but I got a free ticket.

I've climbed inside the Pyramids of Egypt, walked the Via Doloroso in Jerusalem, viewed the Taj Mahal in the moonlight, tracked tigers on elephant-back, sailed the Arabian Sea in search of Halley's Comet and photographed the mountains of Patagonia. All of it has been a great adventure and nothing was a hardship when travel was involved.

Now I live in San Francisco and daydream of a cottage in the West of Ireland. Recently I got out into that country and communed with the sheep and the cows, the pine martens and the badgers, the swans and the migrating Canada geese. I walked along the Flaggy Shore in County Clare, my favorite spot on the planet, where one day someone will scatter my ashes to the wind. I hiked across the Burren, disturbing a herd of wild goats, while for a minute a light snow fell all around me. The Ireland I've loved is still there. The contradictions of the Celtic Tiger can rage all around, and yet I can still find villages like the mythical Brigadoon that come and go with the mist.

My imagined cottage in the West looks out on the wild Atlantic sea, and nearby are some lakes with swans. Sheep graze in the surrounding fields, and in the evening I picture a blazing fire and a couple of cats on my lap. I'm still longing for elsewhere, still experiencing the wanderlust. And just as I daydreamed about China as a child and later realized that dream, I have not given up hope of one day having a wee cottage in Clare or Galway.

There is some energy or spirit, some cellular-level memory that my whole being responds to when I'm on Irish soil. It's something I don't experience anywhere else. Perhaps I'm just caught up in the "endless dreaming" that W.B. Yeats wrote about. I feel akin to those salmon who instinctively, on approaching old age, brave fierce obstacles and treachery to make their way back to the spawning grounds of their birth. To home.